Supporting Windows 7

Addendum to A+ Guide to Managing and Maintaining Your PC, Seventh Edition, and A+ Guide to Software, Fifth Edition

Supporting Windows 7

Addendum to A+ Guide to Managing and Maintaining Your PC, Seventh Edition, and A+ Guide to Software, Fifth Edition

Jean Andrews, Ph.D.

COURSE TECHNOLOGY
CENGAGE Learning

Australia • Brazil • Japan • Korea • Mexico • Singapore • Spain • United Kingdom • United States

COURSE TECHNOLOGY
CENGAGE Learning™

Supporting Windows 7
Jean Andrews

Vice President, Editorial: Dave Garza

Director of Learning Solutions: Matthew Kane

Executive Editor: Stephen Helba

Acquisitions Editor: Nick Lombardi

Managing Editor: Marah Bellegarde

Senior Product Manager: Michelle Ruelos Cannistraci

Developmental Editor: Deb Kaufmann

Editorial Assistant: Sarah Pickering

Vice President, Editorial: Jennifer Baker

Marketing Director: Deborah S. Yarnell

Associate Marketing Manager: Shanna Gibbs

Production Director: Carolyn Miller

Production Manager: Andrew Crouth

Senior Content Project Manager: Andrea Majot

Senior Art Director: Jack Pendleton

Manufacturing Coordinator: Amy Rogers

Compositor: Integra

For product information and technology assistance, contact us at
Cengage Learning Customer & Sales Support, 1-800-354-9706

For permission to use material from this text or product,
submit all requests online at **cengage.com/permissions**
Further permissions questions can be emailed to
permissionrequest@cengage.com

Library of Congress Control Number: 2010938882

ISBN-13: 978-1-111-31707-2
ISBN-10: 1-111-31707-0

Course Technology
25 Channel Center Street
Boston, MA 02210
USA

Some of the product names and company names used in this book have been used for identification purposes only and may be trademarks or registered trademarks of their respective manufacturers and sellers.

Microsoft and the Office logo are either registered trademarks or trademarks of Microsoft Corporation in the United States and/or other countries. Course Technology, a part of Cengage Learning, is an independent entity from the Microsoft Corporation, and not affiliated with Microsoft in any manner.

Course Technology and Course Technology logo are registered trademarks used under license.

Course Technology, a part of Cengage Learning, reserves the right to revise this publication and make changes from time to time in its content without notice.

The programs in this book are for instructional purposes only. They have been tested with care, but are not guaranteed for any particular intent beyond educational purposes. The author and the publisher do not offer any warranties or representations, nor do they accept any liabilities with respect to the programs.

Cengage Learning is a leading provider of customized learning solutions with office locations around the globe, including Singapore, the United Kingdom, Australia, Mexico, Brazil, and Japan. Locate your local office at:
international.cengage.com/region

Cengage Learning products are represented in Canada by Nelson Education, Ltd.

Purchase any of our products at your local college store or at our preferred online store **www.cengagebrain.com**

For your lifelong learning solutions, visit **course.cengage.com**

Visit our corporate website at **cengage.com**.

Printed in the United States of America
2 3 4 5 6 7 12 11

Brief Contents

Table of Contents

Introduction

Supporting Windows 7 contains two new chapters about Microsoft's latest desktop operating system, Windows 7. It is meant to accompany *A+ Guide to Managing and Maintaining Your PC*, Seventh Edition, and *A+ Guide to Software*, Fifth Edition. It builds on the material in these core books and provides an in-depth look at installing, maintaining, securing, and troubleshooting Windows 7. Plenty of screenshots and step-by-step instructions guide students through the process of learning to support this new OS.

For more information about *A+ Guide to Managing and Maintaining Your PC* or *A+ Guide to Software*, please contact your sales representative or go to *www.cengage.com/pcrepair*.

WINDOWS 7 ON THE 2009 A+ EXAMS

CompTIA's 2009 A+ exams will include Windows 7 beginning January, 2011. The revised A+ 2009 objectives showing additional content on Windows 7 are available at CompTIA's Web site (*www.comptia.org*) and also on the Cengage companion site for this book at *www.cengage.com/pcrepair*.

Windows 7 content in Chapter 1 and the beginning of Chapter 2 covers these specific 2009 A+ 220-701 Essentials exam objectives:

Objective Number	Objective	New Windows 7 Objective
3.0	Operating Systems and Software – Unless otherwise noted, operating systems referred to within include Microsoft Windows 2000, Windows XP Professional, XP Home, XP MediaCenter, Windows Vista Home, Home Premium, Business and Ultimate, Windows 7 Starter, Home Premium, Professional and Ultimate	Windows 7 Starter, Home Premium, Professional, and Ultimate
3.1	Compare and contrast the different Windows Operating Systems and their features	Windows 7 32-bit vs. 64-bit Windows OS Upgrade Advisor Microsoft Assessment and Planning Toolkit
3.2	Given a scenario, demonstrate proper use of user interfaces	Libraries in Windows 7
3.3	Explain the process and steps to install and configure the Windows OS	User data migration – User State Migration Tool (USMT)
4.1	Summarize the basics of networking fundamentals, including technologies, devices, and protocols	IPv6 vs. IPv4 ◢ Address length differences ◢ Address conventions

Windows 7 content at the end of Chapter 2 covers these specific 2009 A+ 220-702 Practical Application exam objectives:

Objective Number	Objective	New Windows 7 Objective
2.0	Operating Systems – unless otherwise noted, operating systems referred to within include Microsoft Windows 2000, Windows XP Professional, XP Home, XP MediaCenter, Windows Vista Home, Home Premium, Business and Ultimate, Windows 7 Starter, Home Premium, Professional and Ultimate	Windows 7 Starter, Home Premium, Professional, and Ultimate
2.2	Differentiate between Windows Operating System directory structures ⊿ User file locations ⊿ User profile and program files ⊿ System file locations ⊿ Fonts ⊿ Temporary files ⊿ Program files ⊿ Offline files and folders	Windows 7 directory structure
2.3	Given a scenario, select and use system utilities/tools and evaluate the results	Disk Manager: FAT64 (exFAT) ⊿ External hard drives ⊿ Flash drives
4.2	Implement security and troubleshoot common issues ⊿ Operating systems	Vista/Windows 7 User Account Control (UAC)

FEATURES

To make the book function well for the individual reader as well as in the classroom, you'll find these features:

⊿ **Learning Objectives:** Every chapter opens with a list of Learning Objectives that sets the stage for the goals and content of the chapter.

⊿ **Step-by-Step Instructions:** Detailed information on installation, maintenance, optimization of system performance, and troubleshooting are included throughout the book.

⊿ **End-of-Chapter Material:** Each chapter closes with the following features, which reinforce the material covered in the chapter and provide real-world, hands-on testing of the chapter's skill set:

- **Chapter Summary:** This bulleted list of concise statements summarizes all the major points of the chapter.

- **Key Terms:** The new, important terms introduced in the chapter are defined at the end of the chapter.

- **Reviewing the Basics:** A comprehensive set of review questions at the end of each chapter checks your understanding of fundamental concepts.

- **Thinking Critically:** This section presents you with scenarios that require you to use both real-world common sense and the concepts you've learned in the chapter to solve problems or answer questions.
- **Hands-On Projects:** Several in-depth, hands-on projects are included at the end of each chapter; they are designed to ensure that you not only understand the material, but also can apply what you've learned.
- **Real Problems, Real Solutions:** These projects give you valuable practice in applying the knowledge you've gained in the chapter to real-world situations, often using your own computer or one belonging to someone you know.

◢ **Figures:** Where appropriate, photographs of hardware and screenshots of software are provided to increase student mastery of the topic.

◢ **Notes:** Note icons highlight additional helpful information related to the subject being discussed.

◢ **A+ Icons:** All of the content that relates to CompTIA's 2009 A+ 220-701 Essentials and A+ 220-702 Practical Application certification exams, whether it's a page or a sentence, is highlighted with an A+ icon. The icon notes the exam name and the objective number. This unique feature highlights the relevant content at a glance, so you can pay extra attention to the material.

◢ **A+ Tabs:** Each chapter page is designated with a green A+ Essentials tab or a blue A+ Practical Application tab, allowing the reader to easily identify which exam is relevant to the content on each page.

◢ **Web Site:** For additional content and updates to this book and information about our complete line of CompTIA A+ and PC Repair topics, please visit our Web site at *www.cengage.com/pcrepair.*

INSTRUCTOR RESOURCES

Answers to all end-of-chapter material, including Review Questions and Critical Thinking questions, are provided to instructors online at the textbook's Web site.

Please visit *login.cengage.com* and log in to access instructor-specific recources.

To access additional course materials, please visit *www.cengagebrain.com*. At the *CengageBrain.com* home page, search for the ISBN of your title (from the back cover of your book) using the search box at the top of the page. This will take you to the product page where these resources can be found.

ACKNOWLEDGMENTS

When Microsoft releases a new operating system, we here at Course Technology begin to respond in many ways. Part of that response is making sure that instructors and students have all the materials they need to successfully include the new OS in their curriculum. This book should do just that. The following reviewers all provided invaluable insights and showed a genuine interest in the book's success: Thank you to Michael Avolese, Virginia College, Hunstville, AL; Vincent March, Palomar College, San Marcos, CA; Teresa Sadorus, Lewis-Clark State College, Lewiston, ID; and William Shurbert, Concord Community

College, Concord, NH. Thank you to Deb Kaufmann, the development editor, for your careful attention to details. It has been a pleasure working with you.

This book is dedicated to the covenant of God with man on earth.

— Jean Andrews, Ph.D.

WANT TO CONTACT THE AUTHOR?

Jean's expertise in PC Repair and A+ Certification have been a resource for instructors and students alike for years. Paired with popular social networking sites, Jean is now available to provide feedback to your and your students on anything from PC Repair concepts to certification qualifications for the A+ exams. Visit and interact with Jean at: *http://www.facebook.com/JeanKnows* or *http://twitter.com/jean_andrews*.

If you'd like to give any feedback about the book or suggest what might be included in future books, please feel free to e-mail Jean Andrews at jeanandrews@mindspring.com.

Installing and Maintaining Windows 7

In this chapter, you will learn:

- About new features of Windows 7 and how it differs from Windows Vista
- How to prepare for a Windows 7 installation
- How to install Windows 7, including upgrades, clean installations, and dual-boot systems
- How to use the Windows 7 Action Center to help solve hardware and software problems
- How to use the Windows 7 Backup and Restore utility
- About creating a system image of Windows 7
- About installing and supporting Windows 7 in a large enterprise

Windows 7, Windows Vista, and Windows XP all share the same basic architecture, and they all have similar characteristics. Microsoft considers Windows 7 an upgrade to Windows Vista. Windows 7 has a similar look and feel to Vista, and many utilities first introduced with Vista work the same way in Windows 7. This chapter assumes you already understand how to use, install, and support Windows Vista and assumes you have used Windows 7. Its focus is to show you how supporting Windows 7 differs from supporting Vista. You'll learn about changes to the support tools and methods and how to take full advantage of the improvements made in Windows 7.

In this chapter, you will first learn about the new features of Windows 7, how to prepare for a Windows 7 installation, and the details of installing Windows 7. Then, you'll learn about several of the new or improved utilities for maintaining and supporting Windows 7, including the Action Center, Backup and Restore, and creating a system image. Finally, you'll learn how deploying Windows 7 in a large organization (called an enterprise) differs from manually installing the OS on each computer.

? To Learn More This book is intended to be used as a supplement about Windows 7 to accompany *A+ Guide to Managing and Maintaining Your PC*, 7th Edition, or *A+ Guide to Software*, 5th Edition. These two core textbooks contain many concepts and explanations about the Windows Vista and XP operating systems and how to support them that also apply to Windows 7. See one of these two core books for further explanations and concepts not covered in this book on Windows 7.

Notes Labs to accompany this chapter can be found in Appendix A.

A+ Exam Tip The content in this chapter applies only to the A+ 220-701 Essentials exam.

WHAT'S NEW WITH WINDOWS 7

A+
220-701
3.1, 3.2

Differences in features between Windows 7 and Vista are not as many as between Vista and XP. The Windows 7 user interface, utilities, startup process, and recovery tools are similar to those of Vista. Windows 7, however, generally works faster and uses fewer system resources than does Vista. And the Windows 7 interface is simpler and easier to use. First you'll learn about the improvements Windows 7 has made over Vista, and then about the different Windows 7 versions and editions.

> **Notes** If you have not used Windows 7, you might want to do Lab 1.3 before you read this chapter. The lab gives you practice exploring and customizing Windows 7. Labs for this chapter are found in Appendix A.

WINDOWS 7 IMPROVEMENTS OVER WINDOWS VISTA

Here is a list of the major Windows 7 improvements that users see, and others that a support technician will benefit from when supporting the OS:

▲ *Taskbar changes.* The new and taller taskbar displays a large full-screen preview when you mouse over an open program's icon in the taskbar (see Figure 1-1). When you right-click an icon in the taskbar, the Jump List appears, which provides access to some of the major functions of the program (see Figure 1-2). When you mouse over the rectangle to the far right of the taskbar, all windows disappear so you can see the desktop and any gadgets you might have there (see Figure 1-3). This feature is called Aero Peek because it gives you a peek at the desktop. Click the rectangle to minimize all windows. Click the rectangle again to restore all windows.

Thumbnails of open IE pages

Figure 1-1   Mouse over the Internet Explorer icon in the taskbar to see each open tab in IE
Courtesy: Course Technology/Cengage Learning

> **Notes** Gadgets in Windows 7 can be placed anywhere on the desktop rather than only in the Vista sidebar.

A+
220-701
3.1, 3.2

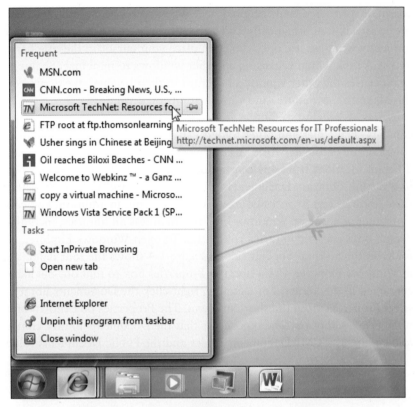

Figure 1-2 Right-click the Internet Explorer icon in the taskbar to see a Jump List of frequently used Web pages and quickly access a page
Courtesy: Course Technology/Cengage Learning

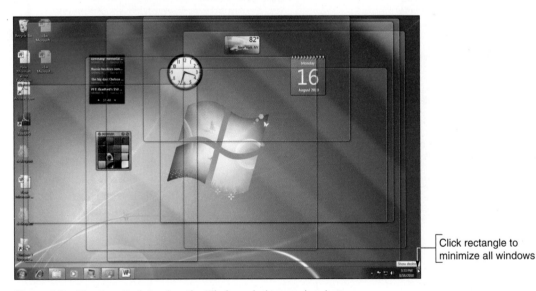

Click rectangle to minimize all windows

Figure 1-3 Use Aero Peek to view the Windows desktop and gadgets
Courtesy: Course Technology/Cengage Learning

▲ *Windows Touch*. Windows Touch allows you to use a touch screen in Windows 7 without additional software. Windows Touch supports multi-touch, which means you can use two fingers to zoom in or out on a screen.

▲ *Snap and shake windows*. Features called Aero Snap and Aero Shake make it easier to manage windows. Aero Snap automatically maximizes a window when you drag it to the top of the desktop. When you drag a window downward that is maximized on the

A+
220-701
3.1, 3.2

screen, it is restored to its original size. When you drag a window to the right or left of the screen, it automatically takes up half the screen size. Using **Aero Shake**, when too many windows are open, you can place your cursor in the title bar of one window and shake the window, causing all other windows to minimize. Shaking the window again causes the other windows to return to their original positions. You can still use the Maximize, Minimize, and Close buttons on a window.

◢ *Libraries*. A Windows 7 *library* is a collection of one or more folders and their contents. These files and other folders can be located in any storage media on the local computer or on the network. A library is a convenient way to access several folders in different locations from one central location. When Windows is installed, it creates four default libraries: Documents, Music, Pictures, and Videos. By default, the first three libraries can be accessed from the Start menu. In addition, you can use the Computer window or Windows Explorer to access all libraries, including the four default ones and any libraries you create. To open Windows Explorer, click the yellow folder in the taskbar. The left side of Figure 1-4 shows the four default libraries listed in Windows Explorer. Use a library's Properties box to find out the locations that are contained in the library. For example, right-click the Documents library and then select **Properties** from the shortcut menu. The Properties box shown on the right side of Figure 1-4 appears. The box shows that the Documents library contains two folders, the user's My Documents folder and the Public Documents folder.

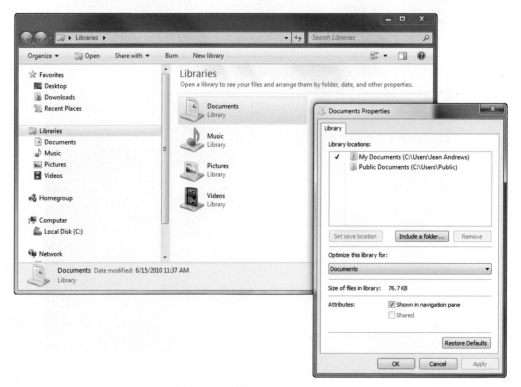

Figure 1-4   Windows 7 includes four default libraries
Courtesy: Course Technology/Cengage Learning

When you add a new folder to a library, the files in that folder appear as though they are in the library even though they continue to be stored in the original location. When you add a file to the library, it is stored in the library's default save location folder. Which folder is that? It's the one checked as the save location in the library's Properties box. For example, in the Properties box shown in Figure 1-4, you can see the check beside the My Documents folder, indicating it is the save location folder.

A+
220-701
3.1, 3.2

📓 **Notes** Lab 1.4 in Appendix A will help you learn to manage a Windows 7 library.

A+
220-701
3.1

▲ *Windows XP Mode.* **Windows XP Mode** allows you to run older applications that are not compatible with Windows 7. The software can be downloaded for free from the Microsoft Web site and runs in a Windows Virtual PC environment. Windows Virtual PC can also be downloaded from Microsoft for free and used with certain editions of Windows 7.

▲ *Action Center.* The Windows 7 **Action Center** replaces the Vista Security Center. It is a centralized location that alerts the user to issues that might need addressing and includes the security issues as well as other issues such as a problem with a scheduled backup. The Action Center flag icon appears in the notification area of the taskbar (see Figure 1-5). Click the icon to see a summary of issues. To open the Action Center, click **Open Action Center** as shown in Figure 1-5. Figure 1-6 shows the Action Center. You will learn to use the Action Center later in the chapter.

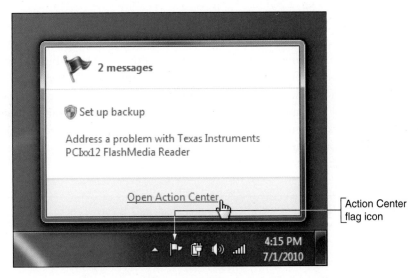

Figure 1-5 Action Center flag in the notification area of the taskbar indicates issues exist
Courtesy: Course Technology/Cengage Learning

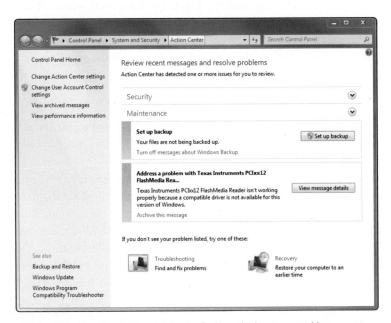

Figure 1-6 Use the Action Center to find a solution to a problem
Courtesy: Course Technology/Cengage Learning

▲ *Homegroups.* In Windows 7 networking, a homegroup is used to share resources on the computer with other computers on the local network that belong to the homegroup. A homegroup works like a workgroup in Vista and XP, but is easier to set up. A homegroup is set up on one Windows 7 PC and assigned a password. Then other Windows 7 computers on the same network (not a domain) can easily join the homegroup when a user enters the homegroup password. At the time the user joins the homegroup, she decides which libraries or folders are shared with other computers in the homegroup. After the computer has joined the homegroup, any user who logs onto the system can access the homegroup resources on the network. The password does not need to be reentered even after the computer is restarted.

Notes Vista and XP do not support homegroups. Therefore, if you want to share Windows 7 resources with Vista or XP computers on the network, you must use a workgroup rather than a homegroup.

▲ *Windows Live Essentials.* Although fundamentally Windows 7 and Vista are the same OS, Microsoft committed to making Windows 7 faster and leaner than Vista. With that goal in mind, some programs are not embedded in the OS but are optional downloads. These Windows Live Essentials programs include Messenger (a chat program), Photo Gallery (to manage photos), Mail (an e-mail client that can handle multiple e-mail accounts), Writer (blogging software), Movie Maker (to create movies and slide shows), Family Safety (to limit online access for specified users), and Toolbar (a search add-on to Internet Explorer). These and other programs can be downloaded for free from the Microsoft Web site, *www.live.com*.

Notes The Family Safety program will not work if Windows 7 is connected to a domain.

▲ *Microsoft Security Essentials.* Microsoft Security Essentials is antivirus software that protects a system against viruses, spyware, rootkits, and other malware. The software can be downloaded for free from the Microsoft Web site at *www.microsoft.com/security_essentials*. Microsoft Security Essentials fares well when rated against other free antivirus software products.

Now let's examine the different editions and versions of Windows 7.

EDITIONS OF WINDOWS 7

Microsoft has produced several editions of Windows 7 designed to satisfy a variety of consumer needs:

▲ Windows 7 Starter has the most limited features and is intended to be used on netbooks or in developing nations. It can only be obtained preinstalled by the manufacturer on a new computer. Windows 7 Starter comes only in the 32-bit version. All other editions of Windows 7 are available in either the 32-bit version or 64-bit version.

▲ Windows 7 Home Basic is designed for low-cost home systems that don't require full security and networking features. It does not use all the features of the Aero user interface.

▲ Windows 7 Home Premium is similar to Windows 7 Home Basic, but includes additional features such as the Aero user interface and Windows DVD Maker. Computers using all editions up through Windows 7 Home Premium cannot join a domain.

A+
220-701
3.1

◢ Windows 7 Professional is intended for business users and is similar to Windows Vista Business. Computers can join a domain, support Group Policy, and use the Encrypted File System for better security. You can also purchase multiple site licenses (also called volume licensing) using this edition.

◢ Windows 7 Enterprise includes additional features over Windows 7 Professional. The major additional features are BitLocker Drive Encryption and support for multiple languages. The edition does not include Windows DVD Maker. Multiple site licensing is available.

◢ Windows 7 Ultimate includes every Windows 7 feature. You cannot purchase multiple licensing with this edition.

> **Notes** An antitrust ruling (a ruling to break up monopolies) in Europe required that Microsoft must offer editions of Windows that do not include multimedia utilities. Windows 7, therefore, comes in N and KN editions that do not include Windows Media Player, Windows Media Center, and Windows DVD Maker. For example, Windows 7 Home Premium N, Windows 7 Ultimate N, and Windows 7 Professional KN do not include these multimedia utilities. If you have an N or KN edition of Windows 7, you can, however, legally download the utilities from the Microsoft Web site.

The major features for all editions are listed in Table 1-1.

Feature	Starter	Home Basic	Home Premium	Professional	Enterprise	Ultimate
Aero user interface			X	X	X	X
Create homegroups			X	X	X	X
Scheduled backups	X	X	X	X	X	X
Backup to network				X	X	X
System image	X	X	X	X	X	X
BitLocker Drive Encryption					X	X
Encrypting File System (EFS)				X	X	X
Windows DVD Maker			X	X		X
Windows Media Center			X	X	X	X
Join a domain				X	X	X
Group Policy				X	X	X
Remote Desktop host				X	X	X
Multiple languages					X	X
Windows XP Mode				X	X	X
Processor: 32-bit or 64-bit		X	X	X	X	X

Table 1-1 Windows 7 editions and their features

> **Notes** Recall that the Windows Vista setup DVD includes all editions of Vista. The edition of Vista that you can install depends on the product key you use. On the other hand, the Windows 7 setup DVD contains only one edition of Windows 7. When you install Windows 7, setup knows which edition to install even if you do not enter the product key during the installation.

A+
220-701
3.1

32-BIT OR 64-BIT VERSIONS

An operating system is built using either 32-bit or 64-bit code. Use a 64-bit version of Windows 7 if you need increased performance and your system has enough resources to support a 64-bit OS. A Windows 7 setup DVD comes with either 32-bit software or 64-bit software installed (see Figure 1-7). When you buy a boxed retail version of Windows 7, both 32-bit and 64-bit DVDs are included.

Figure 1-7   A Windows 7 DVD contains either a 32-bit version or a 64-bit version of Windows
Courtesy: Course Technology/Cengage Learning

> **Notes**   Just as with Vista and XP, a 64-bit installation of Windows 7 installs 64-bit programs in the \Program Files folder and installs 32-bit programs in the \Program Files (x86) folder. Also keep in mind that 64-bit installations of Windows require 64-bit device drivers.

A 64-bit installation of Windows generally runs faster than a 32-bit installation and can support more RAM. Table 1-2 shows how much RAM each edition and version of Windows 7 can support. Another advantage of 64-bit installations of Windows is they can support 64-bit applications, which run faster than 32-bit applications. Even though you can install 32-bit applications in a 64-bit OS, for best performance, always choose 64-bit applications.

Operating System	32-Bit Version	64-Bit Version
Windows 7 Ultimate	4 GB	192 GB
Windows 7 Enterprise	4 GB	192 GB
Windows 7 Professional	4 GB	192 GB
Windows 7 Home Premium	4 GB	16 GB
Windows 7 Home Basic	4 GB	8 GB
Windows 7 Starter	2 GB	NA

Table 1-2   Maximum memory supported by Windows 7 editions and versions

📝 **Notes** How much RAM you can install in a computer depends not only on the OS installed but how much memory the motherboard can hold. To know how much RAM a motherboard can support, see the motherboard documentation.

PREPARING TO INSTALL WINDOWS 7

Before you begin a Windows 7 installation, you need to determine if your hardware resources qualify for Windows 7 and your hardware devices are compatible with Windows 7. Then you need to decide which Windows 7 license you need. If your computer does not have a DVD drive, you need to decide how you will handle that problem. And finally, you need to make several decisions about how Windows will be installed. All these decisions are covered in this part of the chapter.

MINIMUM AND RECOMMENDED HARDWARE REQUIREMENTS

The minimum hardware requirements for Windows 7 are listed in Table 1-3. (These minimum requirements are also Microsoft's recommended requirements.) The requirements are the same as those for Windows Vista. Know, however, that Microsoft occasionally changes the minimum and recommended requirements for an OS.

Hardware	For 32-Bit Windows 7	For 64-Bit Windows 7
Processor	1 GHz or faster	1 GHz or faster
Memory (RAM)	1 GB	2 GB
Free hard drive space	16 GB	20 GB
Video device and driver	DirectX 9 device with WDDM 1.0 or higher driver	DirectX 9 device with WDDM 1.0 or higher driver

Table 1-3   Minimum and recommended hardware requirements for Windows 7

HARDWARE COMPATIBILITY

Many hardware manufacturers have chosen to not produce Windows 7 drivers for their older devices, so it's important to find out if your hardware will be compatible with Windows 7. The simplest way to do that is to download, install, and run the Windows 7 Upgrade Advisor on your computer before you upgrade to Windows 7. You can find the software and instructions on how to use it at *windows.microsoft.com/en-us/windows/downloads/upgrade-advisor.*

Microsoft also offers the Windows 7 Compatibility Center at *www.microsoft.com/windows/compatibility* (see Figure 1-8). You can search under both software and hardware to find out if they are compatible with Windows 7. The site sometimes offers links to patches or fixes for a program or device so that it will work with Windows 7.

If you are not sure that your devices will work under Windows 7, consider setting up a dual boot. A **dual boot** allows you to install the new OS without disturbing the old one so you can boot to either OS. After the installation, you can test your applications and hardware. If they work under the new OS, you can delete the old one. If they don't work, you can still boot to the old OS and use it. How to set up a dual boot is covered later in the chapter.

A+
220-701
3.1, 3.3

Figure 1-8   The Windows 7 Compatibility Center for hardware and software
Courtesy: Course Technology/Cengage Learning

If you have applications written for Windows Vista or XP that are not compatible with Windows 7, you can use compatibility mode or Windows XP Mode in Windows 7 to solve the problem. Compatibility mode is a group of settings that can be applied to older drivers or applications that might cause them to work in Windows 7. Windows XP Mode can also be used to support older applications but might take up additional resources and slow down your system. How to use compatibility mode is covered later in the chapter, and how to set up and use Windows XP Mode is covered in Lab 1.6 in Appendix A of this book.

> **Notes** Before you install a new OS, be sure you have device drivers for all your critical devices such as your network card or motherboard. To find the drivers, look on the CD that came bundled with the device or check the Web site of the device manufacturer.

UPGRADE PATHS FOR WINDOWS 7

Windows 7 can be purchased as an upgrade license or full license. The upgrade license costs considerably less than the full license. Keep these points in mind when deciding which license to purchase:

- You can purchase the less-expensive Windows 7 upgrade license for a PC that already has any Windows XP or Windows Vista license. You are required to purchase the Windows 7 full license for a new computer or any computer that has a Windows 2000 or Windows 9x license.
- Both the Windows 7 full license and upgrade license DVD can be used for a clean installation or in-place upgrade installation of Windows 7. This is true because the Windows 7 setup DVD is the same regardless of the full or upgrade license you purchase. The difference is in the product key, which is tied to the full or upgrade license you purchase. When installing Windows 7, if you use a product key purchased for an upgrade license, setup will verify that the system qualifies to use the upgrade license.

A+
220-701
3.1, 3.3

> **Notes** An **in-place upgrade** is a Windows installation that is launched from the Windows desktop and the installation carries forward user settings and installed applications from the old OS to the new one. A Windows OS is already *in place* before you begin the new installation.
> A **clean install**, also called a **custom installation** in the Windows 7 setup program, creates a fresh installation of Windows and does not carry forward user settings or installed applications.

◢ If you are upgrading Windows XP to Windows 7, Microsoft says you must perform a clean installation and not an in-place upgrade even when you are using an upgrade license. If you are upgrading Windows Vista to Windows 7, sometimes you are allowed to use an in-place upgrade and sometimes you are required to perform a clean installation. Table 1-4 outlines the acceptable upgrade paths for Windows 7.

From OS	To OS
Vista Home Basic	Windows 7 Home Basic, Home Premium, or Ultimate
Vista Home Premium	Windows 7 Home Premium or Ultimate
Vista Business	Windows 7 Professional, Enterprise, or Ultimate
Vista Enterprise	Windows 7 Enterprise
Vista Ultimate	Windows 7 Ultimate
Windows 7 any edition	Can be repaired by performing an in-place upgrade of the same OS
Windows 7 Starter	Anytime upgrade to Windows 7 Home Premium, Professional or Ultimate
Windows 7 Home Basic	Anytime upgrade to Windows 7 Home Premium, Professional or Ultimate
Windows 7 Premium	Anytime upgrade to Windows 7 Professional or Ultimate
Windows 7 Professional	Anytime upgrade to Windows 7 Ultimate

Table 1-4 In-place upgrade paths to Windows 7

In addition to the information given in Table 1-4, keep in mind these tips:

◢ A 64-bit version of Windows can only be upgraded to a 64-bit OS. A 32-bit OS can only be upgraded to a 32-bit OS. If you want to install a 64-bit version of Windows on a computer that already has a 32-bit OS installed, you must perform a clean install.

◢ You can only upgrade Windows Vista to Windows 7 after Vista Service Pack 1 or later has been installed in Vista.

> **? To Learn More** To learn more about choosing the version of Windows to install and the method of installation, see pages 548 through 569 in Chapter 12 of *A+ Guide to Managing and Maintaining Your PC*, 7th edition, or pages 78 through 100 of Chapter 3 of *A+ Guide to Software*, 5th edition.

A+
220-701
3.3

WHEN THE COMPUTER DOES NOT HAVE A DVD DRIVE

Windows 7 normally comes on a DVD, and Windows 7 setup is run from the DVD. Netbooks and some laptops don't have a DVD drive. If the computer does not have a DVD drive, here are some options:

◢ *Use an external DVD drive.* The drive will most likely connect to the PC by way of a USB port. If the PC does not already have an OS installed, you must boot from this

A+
220-701
3.3

USB port. To do so, access BIOS setup and set the boot order for USB as the first boot device. The BIOS setup screen shown in Figure 1-9 shows a removable device as the first boot device. You can then boot from the external DVD drive and install Windows.

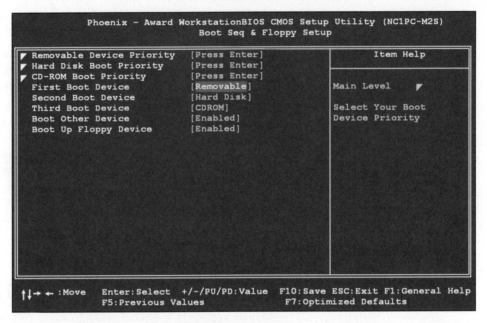

Figure 1-9 Set the boot order in BIOS setup
Courtesy: Course Technology/Cengage Learning

▲ *Download Windows 7 from the Internet.* Purchase Windows 7 on the Internet and download it to your computer's hard drive and install it from there. This option assumes the computer already has a working OS installed.
▲ *Copy setup files on the DVD from another computer on the network that has a DVD drive.* Share the DVD drive on another computer on the network. Then go to the computer that is to receive the Windows installation and locate the DVD drive on the network. Copy the files on the DVD from the other computer across the network to your hard drive. Again, this option assumes the computer already has a working OS installed.
▲ *Perform a network installation of Windows.* Open Windows Explorer and locate the Windows setup DVD made available from another networked computer. Double-click the setup.exe program to run the installation across the network. Again, this option assumes the computer already has a working OS installed.
▲ *Use a USB flash drive.* Using another computer, copy the files on the Windows setup DVD to the USB flash drive. Then use the flash drive to install Windows. If the computer does not already have an OS installed, the USB flash drive must be bootable. Third-party utilities can be used to make a USB flash drive bootable. How to do that is not covered in this book.

CHOOSE THE TYPE OF INSTALLATION: IN-PLACE UPGRADE, CLEAN INSTALL, OR DUAL BOOT

If you are installing Windows on a new hard drive, you must perform a clean install. If an OS is already installed on the hard drive, you have three choices:

▲ *Clean install.* You can perform a clean install, overwriting the existing operating system and applications. During the installation, you will have the option to reformat the hard drive, erasing everything on the drive. After Windows is installed, you will need to install the applications.

▲ *In-place upgrade.* If the upgrade paths allow it, you can perform an in-place upgrade installation. You can upgrade certain editions of Windows Vista to certain editions of Windows 7. Applications and user settings in Vista are carried forward to the new Windows 7 installation. You cannot perform an in-place upgrade from Windows XP to Windows 7.

▲ *Dual boot.* You can install Windows 7 in a second partition and create a dual-boot situation with the other OS. Windows 7/Vista/XP all require that they be the only operating system installed on a partition. So to set up a dual boot, you'll need at least two partitions on the hard drive or a second hard drive.

> **? To Learn More** A clean install, an upgrade, or a dual boot has advantages and disadvantages. To learn more, see page 561 of Chapter 12 of A+ *Guide to Managing and Maintaining Your PC*, 7th edition, or page 91 of Chapter 3 of A+ *Guide to Software*, 5th edition.

INSTALLING WINDOWS 7

In this part of the chapter, you will learn the steps to install Windows 7 as an in-place upgrade, clean install, and dual boot. Let's begin with a few general tips about installing Windows:

▲ If you want to begin the installation by booting from the Windows DVD or other media such as a USB device, use BIOS setup to verify that the boot sequence is first the optical drive or USB device, and then the hard drive.

▲ In BIOS setup, disable any virus protection setting that prevents the boot sector from being altered.

▲ For a notebook computer, connect the AC adapter and use this power source for the complete OS installation, updates, and installation of hardware and applications. You don't want the battery to fail in the middle of the installation process.

▲ Before you begin the installation, back up any data on the hard drive to another media.

Now let's see how to perform an in-place upgrade of Windows Vista to Windows 7.

STEPS TO PERFORMING A WINDOWS 7 IN-PLACE UPGRADE

Recall that an in-place upgrade begins after you have booted the system to the Windows desktop. To upgrade from Windows Vista to Windows 7 carrying applications and user settings forward into the new installation, follow these steps:

1. Close any open applications. Use your antivirus software to scan the system for viruses. After the scan is finished, close the antivirus software so that it does not run in the background. Close any boot management software that might be running in the background. Back up any data on the hard drive that does not have a current backup to another media.

2. Insert the Windows 7 DVD in the DVD drive. You can then launch Windows setup from the AutoPlay dialog box that appears (see Figure 1-10). If it does not appear, enter this command in the Start Search box: **D:\setup.exe**, substituting the drive letter for your DVD drive for D. Respond to the Vista UAC (User Account Control) box.

Figure 1-10   Begin the Windows 7 installation from the AutoPlay box
Courtesy: Course Technology/Cengage Learning

> **Notes**   Figure 1-11 shows the error message that appears when you try to upgrade a 32-bit OS to a 64-bit version of Windows 7.

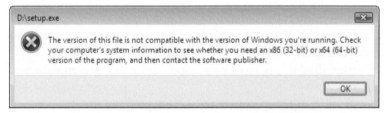

Figure 1-11   Error when running the 64-bit Windows 7 setup program from within a 32-bit operating system
Courtesy: Course Technology/Cengage Learning

3. The opening menu shown in Figure 1-12 appears. If you have not yet performed the Windows 7 Upgrade Advisor process, you can do so now by clicking *Check compatibility online*. To proceed with the installation, click **Install now**.

> **Notes**   If your computer refuses to read from the DVD, verify that your optical drive is a DVD drive. Perhaps it is only a CD drive. If this is the case, you can use another computer on your network that has a DVD drive to read the disc. This computer can act as your file server for the Windows 7 installation on the first PC, or you can copy the installation files on the DVD across the network to a folder on the hard drive of your first PC and install the OS from this folder.

4. On the next screen, you can choose to allow the setup program to download updates for the installation (see Figure 1-13). If you have Internet access, click **Go online to get the latest updates for installation (recommended)**. Setup will download the updates. When using this option, you'll need to stay connected to the Internet throughout the installation.

5. On the next screen, accept the license agreement and click **Next**.

Figure 1-12   Opening menu when you launch Windows 7 setup from within Windows
Courtesy: Course Technology/Cenage Learning

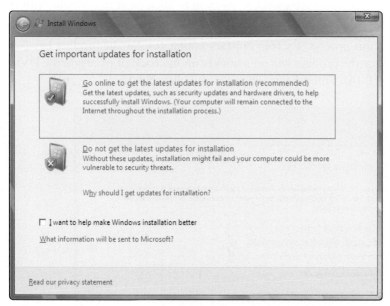

Figure 1-13   Allow setup to download updates for the installation process
Courtesy: Course Technology/Cengage Learning

6. On the next screen, shown in Figure 1-14, select the type of installation you want, either Upgrade or Custom (advanced). The Upgrade option is only available when an existing version of Windows Vista is running. The Custom installation is a clean install. Select **Upgrade**.

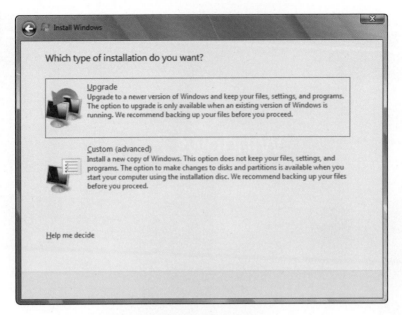

Figure 1-14 Select the type of installation you want
Courtesy: Course Technology/Cengage Learning

7. Setup will check for any compatibility issues. It will verify that the edition of Vista installed can be used as an upgrade path to the edition of Windows 7 you are installing according to the rules outlined earlier in Table 1-4. It will also verify that Windows Vista has a service pack applied. If setup finds a problem, an error message or a warning message appears. An error message requires that you end the installation and resolve the problem. A warning message allows you to click Next to continue with the installation.

8. The installation is now free to move forward. The PC will reboot several times. At the end of this process, a screen appears asking you for the product key (see Figure 1-15). Look for the product key on a sticker on the back of or inside the DVD package (see Figure 1-16). Enter the product key and click **Next**.

Figure 1-15 Enter the product key
Courtesy: Course Technology/Cengage Learning

A+
220-701
3.3

Notes The Windows operating system can be purchased as a retail version or OEM (Original Equipment Manufacturer) version. The OEM version costs less than the retail version, but can only be installed on a new PC for resale.

Product key for
OEM version

Product key for
retail version

Figure 1-16 The Windows 7 product key found on the inside of a retail package or
on the outside of an OEM (Original Equipment Manufacturer) package
Courtesy: Course Technology/Cengage Learning

Notes Notice in Figure 1-15 the checkbox "Automatically activate Windows when I'm online." Normally, you would leave this option checked so that Windows 7 activates immediately. However, if you are practicing installing Windows 7 and intend to install it several times using the same DVD, you might choose to uncheck this box and not enter the product key during the installation. You can later decide to enter the product key and activate Windows after the installation is finished.

9. On the following screen, you are asked how you want to handle Windows updates (see Figure 1-17). Click **Use recommended settings**.

Figure 1-17 Decide how to handle Windows Updates
Courtesy: Course Technology/Cengage Learning

A+
220-701
3.3

10. On the next screen, verify the time and date settings are correct and click **Next**.

11. On the next screen, select the network location (see Figure 1-18). Options are Home network (Network Discovery is turned on and you can join a homegroup), Work network (Network Discovery is turned on and you cannot join a homegroup), and Public network (Network Discovery is turned off and you cannot join a homegroup). Click the option that is appropriate to your network connection. Know that the Public option is the most secure. If you need to change this setting later, do so in the Network and Sharing Center.

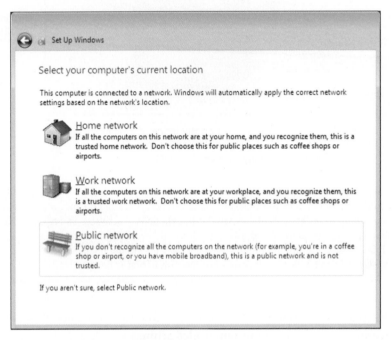

Figure 1-18 Select network settings
Courtesy: Course Technology/Cengage Learning

12. If you selected Home network in the previous step, the screen shown in Figure 1-19 appears, allowing you to configure your homegroup. Check what you want to share with others in your homegroup. If another computer on the network has already assigned a password to the homegroup, enter that password here. In the figure, you are told that the user, Jean Andrews, has assigned this password on the computer BLUELIGHT. Enter the password and click **Next**.

> **Notes** To know what password has been assigned to the homegroup, go to any computer in the homegroup. Open Control Panel and click **Choose homegroup and sharing options** under the Network and Internet group. On the next screen, click **View or print the homegroup password**.

13. Near the end of the installation, Windows Update downloads and installs updates and the system restarts. Finally, a logon screen appears. Log in with your user ID and password. The Windows 7 desktop loads and the installation is complete.

A+
220-701
3.3

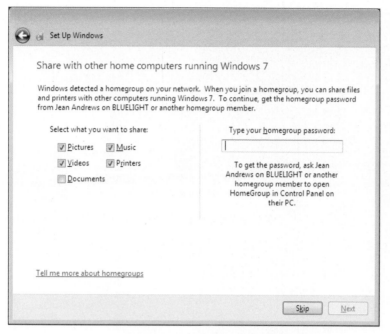

Figure 1-19 Configure your homegroup settings and password
Courtesy: Course Technology/Cengage Learning

STEPS TO PERFORM A CLEAN INSTALL OR DUAL BOOT

To perform a clean install of Windows 7 or a dual boot with another OS, you can begin the installation from the Windows 7 DVD or from the Windows desktop:

▲ If no operating system is installed on the PC, begin the installation by booting from the Windows 7 DVD. Using this method, the Upgrade option is not available and you are forced to do a Custom installation, also called a clean install.

▲ If an operating system is already installed on the PC, you can begin the installation from the Windows desktop or by booting from the Windows 7 DVD. Either way, you can perform a Custom installation. If you are using an upgrade license of Windows 7, setup will verify that a Windows OS is present that qualifies you to use the upgrade license. This is the method to use when upgrading from Windows XP to Windows 7; you are required to perform a clean install even though setup verifies that Windows XP is present.

▲ If you are installing a 64-bit OS when a 32-bit OS is already installed or vice versa, you must begin the installation by booting from the DVD. Setup still allows you to use the less expensive upgrade license even though you are performing a clean install because it is able to verify a Windows installation is present.

Follow these steps to begin the installation by booting from the Windows 7 DVD:

1. Insert the Windows 7 DVD in the DVD drive and start the system, booting directly from the DVD. If you have trouble booting from the disc, go into BIOS setup and verify that your first boot device is the optical drive. On the first screen (see Figure 1-20), select your language and other preferences and click **Next**.

2. The opening menu shown in Figure 1-21 appears. Click **Install now**.

A+
220-701
3.3

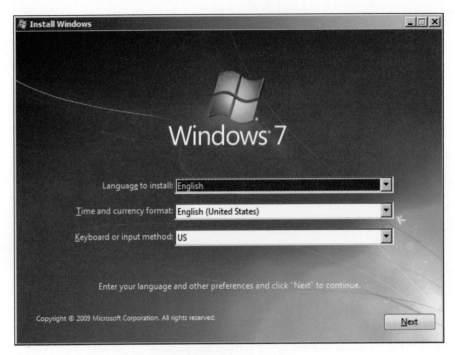

Figure 1-20   Select language, time, and keyboard options
Courtesy: Course Technology/Cengage Learning

Figure 1-21   Screen to begin the Windows 7 installation
Courtesy: Course Technology/Cengage Learning

3. On the next screen, accept the license agreement.

4. On the next screen, shown earlier in Figure 1-14, select the type of installation you want. Choose **Custom (advanced)**.

A+
220-701
3.3

5. On the next screen, you will be shown a list of partitions on which to install the OS. For example, the computer shown in Figure 1-22 has one partition on one hard drive. If you want to use this partition for a clean install, click **Next**, which will cause Windows 7 to replace whatever other OS might be installed on this partition. If you are performing a dual boot and need to create a new partition, click **Drive options (advanced)**; setup will step you through the process of creating a new partition.

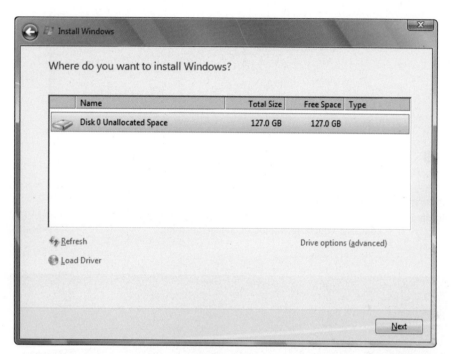

Figure 1-22 Select a partition to install Windows 7 in a clean install or dual-boot environment
Courtesy: Course Technology/Cengage Learning

> **Notes** If you need to shrink a partition to make room for a second partition to hold Windows 7, use Disk Management in Windows Vista to shrink the partition before you begin the Windows 7 installation. You can also use Disk Management to create a new partition to hold the Windows 7 installation and format that partition. The Windows 7 volume must be formatted using the NTFS file system.

6. The installation is now free to move forward. At the end of this process, the window in Figure 1-23 appears asking for a user name and computer name. Enter these values and click **Next**. On the next screen, you can enter a password for your user account by entering the password twice followed by a password hint. Then, click **Next**.

7. The installation now continues the same way as an upgrade installation. You are asked to enter the product key, Windows update settings, time and date settings, and network settings. Windows Update downloads and installs updates and you are asked to restart the system. After the restart, the logon screen appears. After you log in, the Windows 7 desktop loads (see Figure 1-24) and the installation is complete.

A+
220-701
3.3

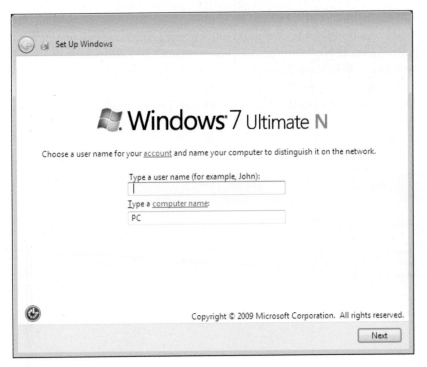

Figure 1-23   Choose a user name and computer name
Courtesy: Course Technology/Cengage Learning

Figure 1-24   The Windows 7 desktop shows updates in progress
Courtesy: Course Technology/Cengage Learning

After the installation, when you boot with a dual boot, the boot loader menu automatically appears and asks you to select an operating system, as shown in Figure 1-25.

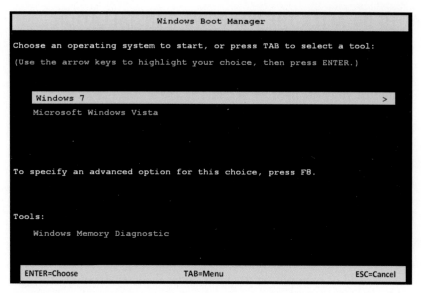

```
                        Windows Boot Manager

Choose an operating system to start, or press TAB to select a tool:

(Use the arrow keys to highlight your choice, then press ENTER.)


  Windows 7                                                      >
  Microsoft Windows Vista




To specify an advanced option for this choice, press F8.



Tools:

  Windows Memory Diagnostic



  ENTER=Choose              TAB=Menu                 ESC=Cancel
```

Figure 1-25   Boot loader menu in a dual-boot environment
Courtesy: Course Technology/Cengage Learning

When using a dual boot, you can execute an application while Windows 7 or Vista is loaded even if the application is installed under the other OS. If the application is not listed in the Start menu, locate the program file in Windows Explorer. Double-click the application to run it from Windows 7 or Vista. You do not have to install an application twice under each OS.

USING THE WINDOWS 7 UPGRADE DVD ON A NEW HARD DRIVE

Windows 7 setup expects that an old OS is installed if you use the upgrade license DVD. This requirement presents a problem when you are replacing a hard drive. You have two options in this situation:

◢ Install Vista or XP first and then install Windows 7. You must also install a service pack under Vista or XP before you install Windows 7. This first option takes a long time!

◢ Install Windows 7 twice. Follow these steps:

1. Use the Windows 7 upgrade DVD to perform a clean install. When you get to the installation window that asks you to enter your product key, don't enter the key and uncheck **Automatically activate Windows when I'm online**. Complete the installation.

2. From the Windows 7 desktop, start the installation routine again, but this time as an upgrade. Enter the product key during the installation and Windows 7 will activate with no problems.

> **Notes** If you have problems installing Windows, search the Microsoft Web site (*support.microsoft.com*) for solutions. Windows 7 setup creates several log files during the installation that can help you solve a problem. The list can be found in the Microsoft Knowledge Base Article 927521 at this link: *support.microsoft.com/kb/927521*.

A+
220-701
3.3

WHAT TO DO AFTER THE WINDOWS 7 INSTALLATION

After you have installed Windows 7, you need to do the following:

- ◢ For an OEM installation, affix the product key sticker to the computer.
- ◢ Verify that you have network access.
- ◢ Activate Windows.
- ◢ Install updates and service packs for Windows.
- ◢ Verify automatic updates are set as you want them.
- ◢ Install hardware.
- ◢ Install applications.
- ◢ Turn Windows features on or off.
- ◢ For a laptop, configure power management settings.

If Windows is installed in a homegroup and not a domain, in addition to these nine steps, you need to create a local user account for each user of this PC. To create a local user account, click **Add or remove user accounts** under the User Accounts and Family Safety group of Control Panel. You can transfer user settings and user data from an old computer to this new installation of Windows using Windows Easy Transfer or the User State Migration Tool. Both tools work as they do in Vista.

Now let's look at the details of the nine items from the preceding list.

> **? To Learn More** To learn more about what to do after you have installed Windows, see pages 576 through 587 in Chapter 12 of *A+ Guide to Managing and Maintaining Your PC,* 7th edition, or pages 107 through 118 in Chapter 3 of *A+ Guide to Software,* 5th edition.

AFFIX THE CERTIFICATE OF AUTHENTICITY TO THE CASE OF A NEW COMPUTER

The OEM (Original Equipment Manufacturer) version of Windows 7 comes with a sticker, called the **Certificate of Authenticity**, which is attached to the outside of the DVD case. Microsoft requires you paste the sticker, which includes the product key, to the exterior of the PC (see Figure 1-26). Affix the sticker to the side or rear of a desktop computer or the bottom of a laptop.

Figure 1-26   Paste the Windows 7 Certificate of Authenticity sticker to a new desktop
Courtesy: Course Technology/Cengage Learning

VERIFY THAT YOU HAVE NETWORK ACCESS

When you install Windows, the setup process should connect you to the network and to the Internet, if available. To verify that you have network and Internet access, do the following:

1. Click the **Windows Explorer** icon (yellow folder) in the taskbar. Windows Explorer opens (see Figure 1-27). If other computers are turned on and available to the network, you should see these computers and resources on the network in the right pane of Windows Explorer. Try to drill down to see shared resources on these computers.

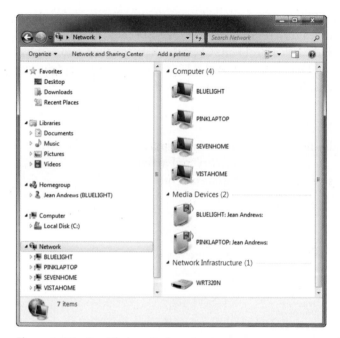

Figure 1-27 Use Windows Explorer to access resources on your network
Courtesy: Course Technology/Cengage Learning

2. To verify that you have Internet access, open **Internet Explorer** and try to navigate to a couple of Web sites.

If the Explorer window does not show other computers on your network or you cannot access the Internet, do the following to troubleshoot the problem:

1. Check the networking icon in the taskbar for errors. Local wired networks will show the icon on the left side of Figure 1-28 and wireless networks show the icon on the right side of Figure 1-28. An icon that indicates a problem is shown in Figure 1-29. To get more information about the problem, click **Open Network and Sharing Center** in the Not connected box.

Figure 1-28 Wired and wireless networking icons in the taskbar
Courtesy: Course Technology/Cengage Learning

A+
220-701
1.1, 2.2,
3.2

Figure 1-29 The network icon in the taskbar indicates a problem
Courtesy: Course Technology/Cengage Learning

2. The Network and Sharing Center window opens (see Figure 1-30). Items in this window are arranged differently from that of Vista, but the center functions the same way. The red X indicates a problem. Click the X to get help and resolve the problem. Windows Network Diagnostics starts looking for problems, applying solutions, and making suggestions. You can also check these things:

◢ Is the network cable connected?
◢ Are status light indicators on the network port and router or switch lit or blinking appropriately to indicate connectivity and activity?
◢ Is the wireless switch on a laptop turned on?

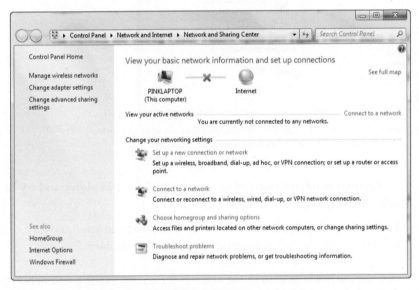

Figure 1-30 The Network and Sharing Center reports a problem connecting to the network
Courtesy: Course Technology/Cengage Learning

3. After Windows has resolved the problem, you should see a clear path from the computer to the Internet as shown in Figure 1-31. Use Windows Explorer to try again to access resources on the local network, and use Internet Explorer to try to access the Internet.

A+
220-701
1.1, 2.2,
3.2

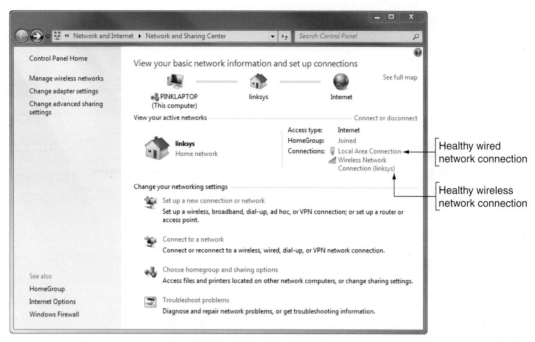

Figure 1-31 The Network and Sharing Center reports two healthy network connections
Courtesy: Course Technology/Cengage Learning

If you still do not have local or Internet access, it's time to dig a little deeper into the source of the problem. Let's consider the following problems and their solutions.

A+
220-701
1.1, 2.2,
3.2, 4.1,
4.3

Wireless Security Settings Are Wrong

Maybe there is a problem with the security settings for secured wireless network. To view and change these settings, follow these steps:

1. In the left pane of the Network and Sharing Center, click **Manage wireless networks**. The Manage Wireless Networks window appears (see the left side of Figure 1-32).

2. Using this window, you can change the order of networks that Windows uses to try to make a wireless connection. To view security settings, double-click a network in the list. The Properties box for the wireless network appears.

3. On the Properties box, click the **Security** tab, which is shown in the right side of Figure 1-32. Check **Show characters** so that you can verify the Network security key is correct. Windows 7 should automatically sense the Security type and Encryption type for the wireless network and these values should be correct. Change the Network security key if necessary.

4. Click **OK** to close the Properties box. Windows should automatically connect to the network.

A+
220-701
1.1, 2.2,
3.2, 4.1,
4.3

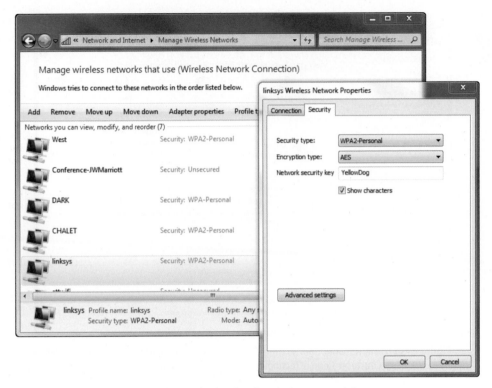

Figure 1-32 Verify the Network security key for the wireless network is correct
Courtesy: Course Technology/Cengage Learning

TCP/IP Settings Are Wrong

Perhaps TCP/IP settings are wrong. To verify these settings, follow these steps:

1. In the Network and Sharing Center window, click the connection. For example, in Figure 1-31, click **Local Area Connection**. The Local Area Connection Status box opens (see the left side of Figure 1-33). Click **Properties**. The Properties box for the connection opens (see the middle of Figure 1-33).

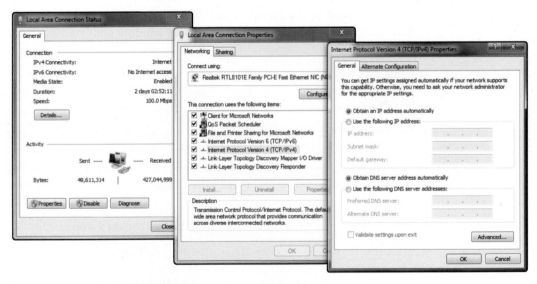

Figure 1-33 Configure TCP/IP settings
Courtesy: Course Technology/Cengage Learning

A+
220-701
1.1, 2.2,
3.2, 4.1,
4.3

2. Select the TCP/IP version you are using. For most situations, you will select **Internet Protocol Version 4 (TCP/IPv4)**. Then click **Properties**. The TCP/IP Properties box opens as shown on the right side of Figure 1-33.

3. If your network is using dynamic IP addressing, leave the settings as shown in the figure as **Obtain an IP address automatically**. If your network is using static IP addressing, select **Use the following IP address** and enter the IP address, subnet mask, and default gateway. You can also enter DNS server IP addresses if you have that information available.

4. Click **OK** twice to close both Property boxes. Then close the connection status box.

> **Notes** For laptop computers that move from one network to another and a particular network uses static IP addressing, select **Obtain an IP address automatically** in the TCP/IP Properties box. Then click the **Alternate Configuration** tab where you can enter the static IP address settings. The laptop will first attempt to obtain an IP address from the DHCP server. If it cannot, it will then apply the static IP address configuration you provided.

A+
220-701
1.1, 2.2,
3.2

Homegroup Settings Are Wrong

If you still have problems accessing resources on the local network, the problem might be with homegroup settings when connected to a Home network. Follow these steps to solve the problem:

1. Have you joined the computer to a homegroup? To verify, click **Start** and type **homegroup** in the Search programs and files box and press **Enter**. The HomeGroup window opens. Figure 1-34 shows the window when the computer has not been joined to a homegroup.

Figure 1-34   The computer has not been joined to a homegroup
Courtesy: Course Technology/Cengage Learning

2. Click **Join now**. On the next screen, select the type of files to share in the homegroup and click **Next**. On the next window, enter the homegroup password and click **Next**. Then click **Finish**. Figure 1-35 shows the HomeGroup window as it appears when the computer is joined. Verify the correct type files are shared. If you make changes to this window, click **Save changes** to close the window. Otherwise, click **Cancel**.

A+
220-701
1.1, 2.2,
3.2

Notes To know what password has been assigned to the homegroup, do the following: Go to any computer on the network that belongs to the homegroup, open Control Panel, and click **Choose homegroup and sharing options** under the Network and Internet group. On the next screen, click **View or print the homegroup password.**

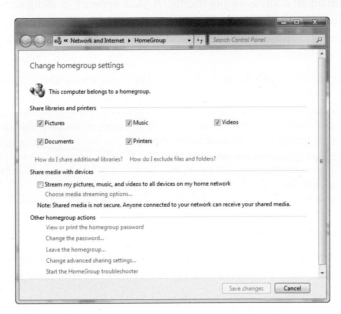

Figure 1-35 The computer has not been joined to a homegroup
Courtesy: Course Technology/Cengage Learning

Network Discovery Settings Are Wrong

The next settings to check are network discovery settings. Follow these steps:

1. In the Network and Sharing Center left pane, click **Change advanced sharing settings** (refer back to Figure 1-31). The Advanced sharing settings window opens (see Figure 1-36).

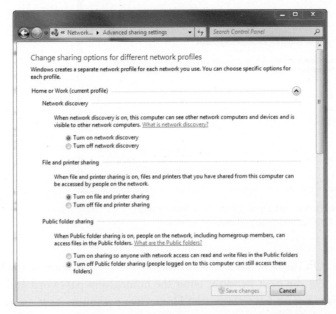

Figure 1-36 Network discovery settings and other network settings
Courtesy: Course Technology/Cengage Learning

A+
220-701
1.1, 2.2,
3.2

2. Two categories of settings in the window are Home or Work (near the top of the window) and Public (near the bottom of the window). The current profile in Figure 1-36 is the Home or Work profile. To see the Public profile settings, scroll down to the bottom of the window and click the down arrow to the right of Public. To return to the Home or Work profile, scroll up toward the top of the window and click the down arrow to the right of Home or Work.

3. In the Home or Work profile, verify that **Turn on network discovery** is selected and **Turn on file and printer sharing** is selected.

4. The next setting is for Public folder sharing. If you want others on the network to have access to the Public folder, select **Turn on sharing so anyone with network access can read and write files in the Public folders.**

Problems with Accessing Resources on Vista or XP Systems

Are you trying to share network resources with a Vista or XP computer on the network? If so, you might need to switch from Windows 7 managing a homegroup to manually managing share permissions to be compatible with Vista and XP. Follow these steps:

1. Scroll down to the HomeGroup connections setting (see Figure 1-37). Select **Use user accounts and passwords to connect to other computers.** Sharing files and folders on the network will now work following the methods used in Vista and XP. Each user on the network must have a user account and password that matches one on this computer to access its resources.

> **? To Learn More** For a detailed discussion of how to share files and folders on a network, see pages 1040 through 1048 of Chapter 20 in *A+ Guide to Managing and Maintaining Your PC*, 7th edition, and pages 546 through 570 of Chapter 11 of *A+ Guide to Software*, 5th edition.

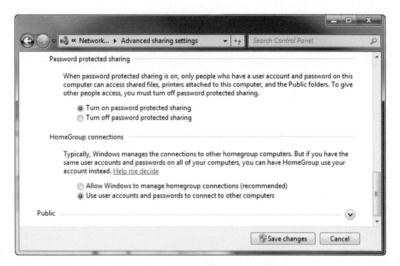

Figure 1-37 Control how shared resources are managed
Courtesy: Course Technology/Cengage Learning

2. If you want to allow users to access resources on this computer who do not have a user account and password on this computer, in the Password protected sharing setting shown in Figure 1-37, select **Turn off password protected sharing.**

A+
220-701
1.1, 2.2,
3.2

3. After you have made all your changes, click **Save changes** to close the Advanced sharing settings window.

Do You Need to Join a Domain?

Perhaps you are working on a computer in a corporate environment and the computer must join the domain that is securing the network. Follow these steps to join the computer to a domain:

1. Click the **Start** button, right-click **Computer**, and select **Properties** from the shortcut menu. The System window opens (see the left side of Figure 1-38).

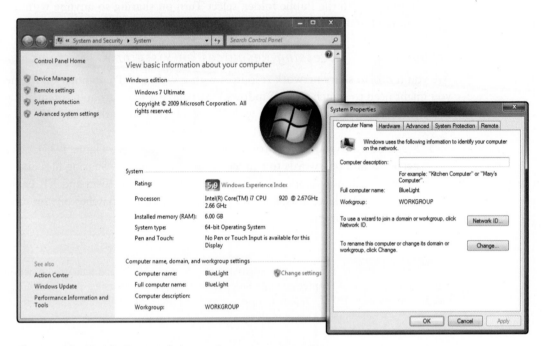

Figure 1-38 Use the System window to change computer settings
Courtesy: Course Technology/Cengage Learning

2. Scroll down to the *Computer name, domain, and workgroup settings* group. Click **Change settings**. The System Properties dialog box displays as shown in the right side of Figure 1-38. (If you are installing a Windows 7 Home edition, the Network ID button in the figure will be missing because these editions cannot join a domain.)

3. To join a domain, click **Network ID** and follow the directions on-screen to join the domain. To join the domain, you will need your user name and password on the domain, the computer name, and the name of the domain. Your network administration will have all that information. You will need to restart the computer before your changes will take effect.

> **Notes** If your Windows 7 computer is part of a Windows domain but you want to log onto the local computer, on the Welcome screen, click **Switch User**. Then click **Other User**. In the user name area, type the name of the computer and your local user account separated with a backslash like this: **mycomputer\Jean Andrews**. Then type your password and press **Enter**.

ACTIVATE WINDOWS 7

If you don't activate Windows 7 during the installation, you have 30 days to do so. To view the activation status and product key, open the System window. From this window, you can also change the product key before you activate the installation.

If you change the key after Windows is activated, you must activate Windows again, because the activation is tied to the product key and the system hardware. Incidentally, if you replace the motherboard or replace the hard drive and memory at the same time, you must also reactivate Windows.

To activate Windows 7, click the **Start** button and enter **activate** in the Search programs and files box and press **Enter**. The Windows Activation window opens (see Figure 1-39). Click **Activate Windows online now** to begin the process. If you have not yet entered a product key, the next screen allows you to do that.

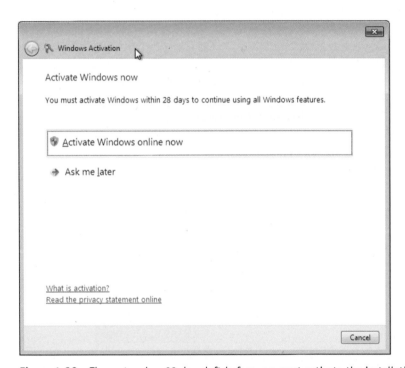

Figure 1-39   The system has 28 days left before you must activate the installation
Courtesy: Course Technology/Cengage Learning

INSTALL WINDOWS UPDATES AND SERVICE PACKS

The Microsoft Web site offers patches, fixes, and updates for known problems and has an extensive knowledge base documenting problems and their solutions. It's important to keep these updates current on your system to fix known problems and plug up security holes that might allow viruses and worms in. Be sure to install updates before you attempt to install software or hardware.

To download and apply Windows updates, click **Start, All Programs,** and **Windows Update**. The Windows Update window appears as shown in Figure 1-40. Click **Install updates** and follow the directions on-screen.

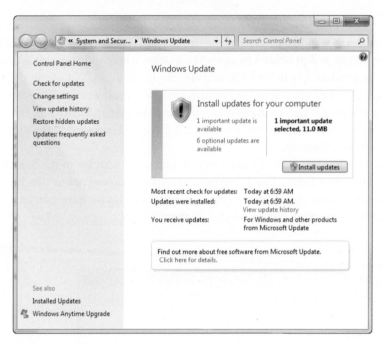

Figure 1-40 Download and install updates for your computer
Courtesy: Course Technology/Cengage Learning

CONFIGURE AUTOMATIC UPDATES

During the Windows installation, you were asked how you want to handle Windows updates. To verify or change this setting, in the left pane of the Windows Update window, click **Change settings**. From the Change settings window, shown in Figure 1-41, you can decide how often, when, and how you want Windows to install updates. The recommended setting is to allow Windows to automatically download and install updates daily. However, if you are not always connected to the Internet, your connection is very slow, or you want more control over which updates are installed, you might want to manage the updates differently.

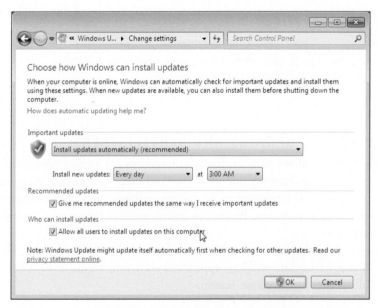

Figure 1-41 Manage how and when Windows is updated
Courtesy: Course Technology/Cengage Learning

INSTALL HARDWARE

You're now ready to install the hardware devices that were not automatically installed during the installation. As you install each device, reboot and verify that the device is working before you move on to the next item. Hardware installations work as they do in Vista, so the details will not be repeated here.

> **? To Learn More** To learn more about hardware installations, see pages 582 through 583 of Chapter 12 of *A+ Guide to Managing and Maintaining Your PC*, 7th edition, or pages 113 through 114 of Chapter 3 of *A+ Guide to Software*, 5th edition.

If you have a problem with an installation, as with Vista, begin troubleshooting by checking Device Manager for errors. Windows 7 offers another tool you can use to solve hardware problems: the Action Center. The Action Center can easily take you to the Problem Reports window that offers solutions for both hardware and application problems.

Let's look at a couple of problems you might run into when installing hardware and see how Windows 7 handles them.

When the Driver for a USB Device Is Not Present

Installing a USB device is generally very easy: Plug in the device and Windows installs it. Figure 1-42 shows the error message window that appeared when a USB keyboard and USB printer were connected to a computer following a Windows 7 installation.

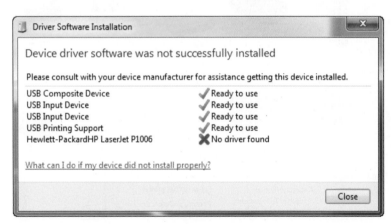

Figure 1-42 Windows 7 reports a problem with a driver for a USB printer
Courtesy: Course Technology/Cengage Learning

Immediately after this first window appeared, the window in Figure 1-43 appeared. When the user clicked **Click to download and install the new driver from the Hewlett-Packard Company website**, the driver was immediately downloaded and installed with no errors.

To see the list of installed printers and verify the printer installed correctly, follow these steps:

1. Click **Start** and then click **Devices and Printers**. The Devices and Printers window opens.

2. To print a test page, right-click the printer and select **Printer properties** from the shortcut menu. Incidentally, notice in the shortcut menu shown in Figure 1-44 other important options you might need when supporting printers, which include *See what's printing* (to view and manage the print queue), *Set as default printer*, and *Printing preferences*.

A+
220-701
2.2, 2.3

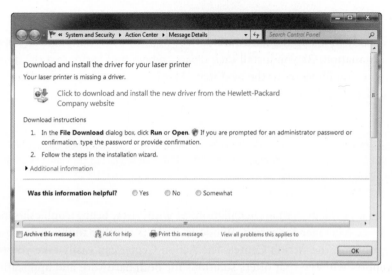

Figure 1-43 Windows offers to find the missing USB printer driver
Courtesy: Course Technology/Cengage Learning

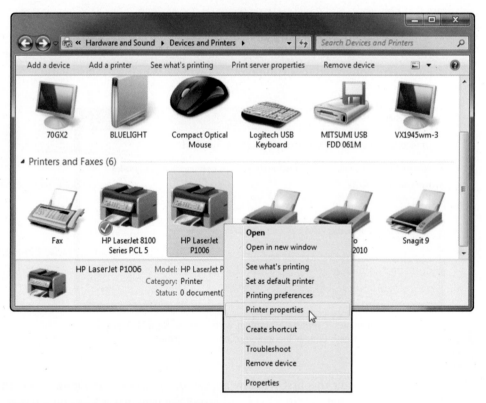

Figure 1-44 Installed devices and printers
Courtesy: Course Technology/Cengage Learning

3. The Properties box shown in Figure 1-45 appears when you click Printer properties on the printer's shortcut menu. Click **Print Test Page** to send a page to the printer and verify that the printer is working correctly.

Use the Devices and Printers window and the printer Properties box to solve problems with a stalled print spool and a corrupted or incompatible print driver.

A+
220-701
2.2, 2.3

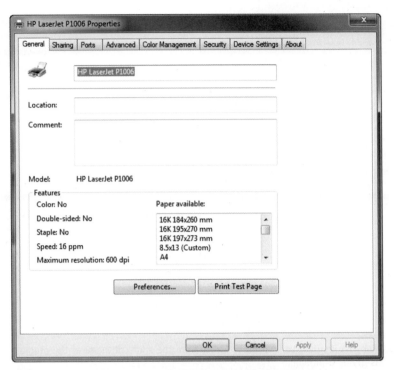

Figure 1-45   Print a test page from the printer's Properties box
Courtesy: Course Technology/Cengage Learning

When a Windows 7 Driver Is Not Available

Older hardware devices might present a problem. A Windows Vista driver is likely to work in the Windows 7 installation because Vista and Windows 7 are so closely related. If the driver does not load correctly or gives errors, first search the Internet for a Windows 7 driver. If you don't find one, try running the Vista driver installation program in compatibility mode. Recall that compatibility mode is a group of settings that can be applied to older drivers or applications that might enable them to work in Windows 7.

In the example that follows, we're using the installation program for a memory card reader/writer that worked under Vista, but did not load correctly when we installed Windows 7. Follow these steps to use compatibility mode with the driver installation program:

1. Using Windows Explorer, locate the program file with an .exe file extension for the driver installation program. Right-click the program file and select **Troubleshoot compatibility** from the shortcut menu (see Figure 1-46). The Program Compatibility utility launches.

2. On the first screen of the troubleshooter utility (see Figure 1-47), select **Troubleshoot program.**

3. On the next screen, check the problems that apply (see Figure 1-48). In the example, the driver worked fine in Windows Vista, so select **The program worked in earlier versions of Windows but won't install or run now.** Click **Next.**

4. On the next screen, the troubleshooter asks for the OS with which the program worked (see Figure 1-49). For this example, you would select **Windows Vista (Service Pack 2)** and click **Next.**

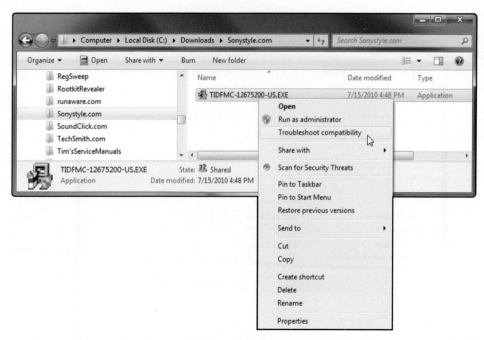

Figure 1-46 Run the Program Compatibility utility from the shortcut menu of the program that is giving a problem
Courtesy: Course Technology/Cengage Learning

Figure 1-47 Troubleshoot the problem with the legacy installation program
Courtesy: Course Technology/Cengage Learning

5. On the next screen, click **Start the program** and respond to the UAC box. The program runs and successfully installs the drivers for the memory card device. Checking Device Manager shows no errors with the device. When you test the device, it can both read and write data to a memory card. Compatibility mode worked for this particular driver.

A+
220-701
2.2, 2.3

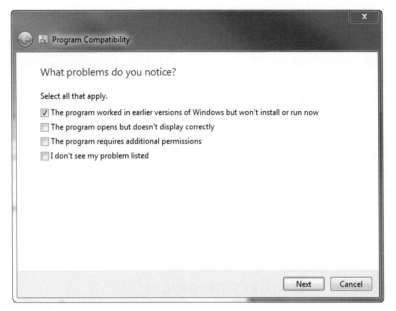

Figure 1-48 Select all the problems that apply
Courtesy: Course Technology/Cengage Learning

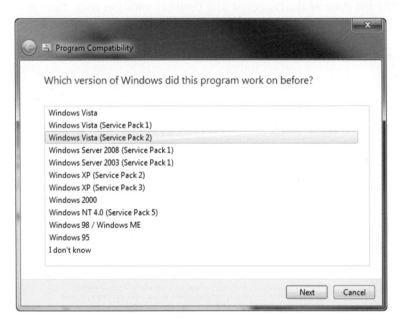

Figure 1-49 Select the operating system with which the program worked
Courtesy: Course Technology/Cengage Learning

A+
220-701
2.2

INSTALL APPLICATIONS

Software installations also work as they do in Vista and so the details are not repeated here.

> **? To Learn More** To learn more about installing software, see pages 583 through 587 in Chapter 12 of *A+ Guide to Managing and Maintaining Your PC,* 7th edition, or pages 114 through 118 of Chapter 3 of *A+ Guide to Software,* 5th edition.

A+
220-701
2.2

If you have a problem with an older application not working in Windows 7, here are some steps you can take:

1. Check the Web site of the software manufacturer and the Microsoft support site (*support.microsoft.com*) for solutions. Search on the application name or the error message you get when you try to run it. Perhaps the manufacturer offers a patch to fix the problem or an upgrade release of the application.

2. Try running the application in compatibility mode. The best way to start the process is to follow the steps given earlier under the chapter section *Install Hardware*. You can also begin compatibility mode as is done in Vista by right-clicking the program file and selecting **Properties** from the shortcut menu. Then select the **Compatibility** tab.

3. If compatibility mode does not work, try Windows XP Mode. Windows XP Mode creates a virtual machine environment similar to Windows XP. The detailed steps of setting up and using Windows XP Mode are covered in Lab 1.6 in Appendix A of this book.

TURN WINDOWS 7 FEATURES ON OR OFF

You can save on system resources by turning off Windows features you will not use, and you might need to turn on some features that are, by default, turned off. To control Windows features, open **Control Panel** and click **Uninstall a program** in the Programs group. In the left pane of the Programs and Features window, click **Turn Windows features on or off**. Check or uncheck the features you want or don't want and then click **OK**.

> **Notes** The Programs and Features window can also be used to uninstall or change an installed program. To do so, select the program and then click the appropriate link at the top of the list.

A+
220-701
1.10

CONFIGURE POWER MANAGEMENT SETTINGS ON A LAPTOP

For laptops, verify the power management settings are as you want them. To view and change these settings, in Control Panel, click **Hardware and Sound**. In the Hardware and Sound window, click **Power Options**. The Power Options window opens as shown in Figure 1-50. Make

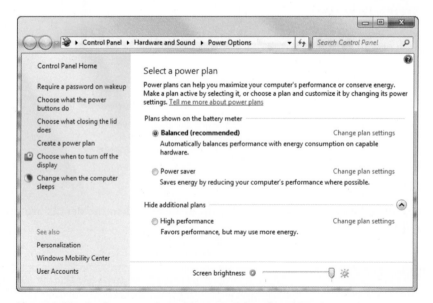

Figure 1-50 Configure power management settings for a laptop
Courtesy: Course Technology/Cengage Learning

A+
220-701
1.10

your adjustments to control power to the laptop including when the laptop goes into sleep or hibernate mode to conserve power and then close the window.

You should now have Windows 7 configured and functioning as you want it. To finish up, do one last restart and verify that everything is working and looking good. After you have verified everything, it's a good idea to back up the entire volume on which Windows 7 is installed. This backup is called a system image. How to create a system image is covered later in the chapter.

WINDOWS 7 ACTION CENTER

A+
220-701
2.5, 3.2,
3.3

Almost all the support tools used to maintain and troubleshoot Vista can be found in Windows 7 and work the same way, although some of the tools have been renamed in Windows 7. One new tool in Windows 7 is the Action Center, a window that gives you an easy-to-access central location to find many of these support tools. In this part of the chapter, you will learn to use the Action Center.

To open the Action Center, use one of these methods:

◢ Click the **flag icon** in the taskbar and click **Open Action Center** in the box that appears. If the flag has a red X beside it as shown in Figure 1-51, Windows considers the system has an important issue that needs resolving immediately.

Figure 1-51 A red X on the Action Center icon in the taskbar indicates that a critical issue needs resolving
Courtesy: Course Technology/Cengage Learning

◢ Click **Start** and type **Action Center** in the Search programs and files box and press **Enter**.
◢ Click **Start** and then click **Control Panel**. The Control Panel opens. Under the System and Security group, click **Review your computer's status**.

Using either method, the Action Center for one computer shown in Figure 1-52 appears. Notice the colored bar to the left of a problem. The red color indicates a critical problem that needs immediate attention. In this example, antivirus software is not installed on the system. The orange color indicates a less critical problem, such as no backups are scheduled. Click the button to the right of a problem to find a recommended solution.

Now let's take a closer look at some of the tools available in the Action Center.

PROBLEMS AND SOLUTIONS REPORTED IN THE ACTION CENTER

When you first open the Action Center, any problem that needs addressing is displayed. Looking back at Figure 1-6 shown earlier in the chapter, you can see the Action Center reports a problem in the Maintenance group with a Texas Instruments FlashMedia Reader. When you click **View message details**, the screen shown in Figure 1-53 appears. This window looks and works like the Vista Problem Reports and Solutions window. Looking at Figure 1-53, you can see that the device does not have a Windows 7 driver and Windows is

A+
220-701
2.5, 3.2,
3.3

Figure 1-52 The Action Center shows a critical problem that needs a resolution
Courtesy: Course Technology/Cengage Learning

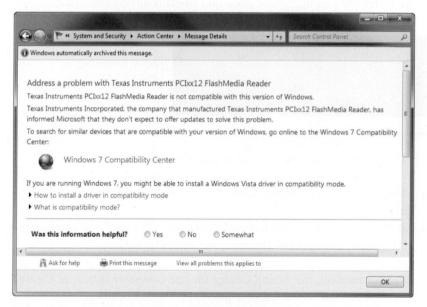

Figure 1-53 A problem reported in the Action Center with a possible solution
Courtesy: Course Technology/Cengage Learning

suggesting the problem might be solved by installing a Vista driver using compatibility mode. By clicking the links on the window, you can attempt the solution. To view a history of prior error messages shown in the Action Center, click **View archived messages** in the left pane of the Action Center (refer to Figure 1-52).

The Action Center only lists problems when solutions are available. To see a complete list of past and current problems on this computer, click **Start**, type **view all problem reports** in the Search programs and files box, and press **Enter**. The window shown in Figure 1-54 appears. This report helps understand the history of problems on a computer that you are troubleshooting. The problems in this list might or might not have a solution.

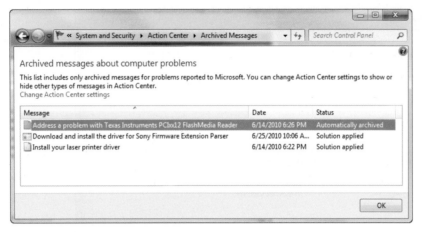

Figure 1-54 A list of archived messages that might have a solution
Courtesy: Course Technology/Cengage Learning

SECURITY AND MAINTENANCE SETTINGS AND SUPPORT TOOLS

To see other information available under the Security and Maintenance groups, click the down arrow to the right of a group. For example, after the arrow to the right of Security is clicked, detailed information about Windows Firewall, Windows Update, and other security settings appears, as shown in Figure 1-55.

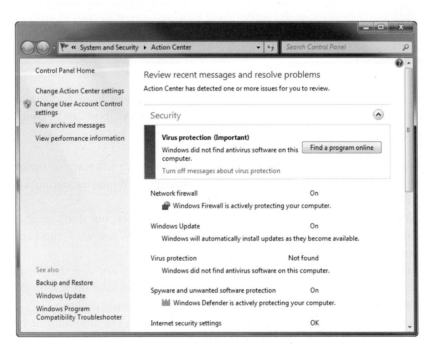

Figure 1-55 View detailed information about security settings
Courtesy: Course Technology/Cengage Learning

You can easily access support tools from links in the left pane of the Action Center window and at the bottom of the window. For example, when you click **Change User Account Control settings** in the left pane of the Action Center window, you can change how the UAC box works (see Figure 1-56).

A+
220-701
2.5, 3.2,
3.3

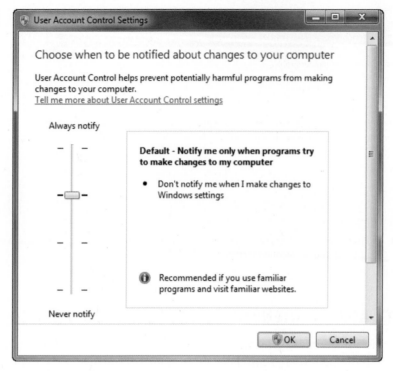

Figure 1-56   Control how the UAC box works in Windows 7
Courtesy: Course Technology/Cengage Learning

Notes The UAC (User Account Control) box in Windows 7 does not appear as often as it does in Vista. For example, even if the UAC box is turned on, an administrator can change the system date or time and a standard user can install Windows updates without the UAC box appearing.

Windows 7 offers more control over the UAC box than does Vista. In Vista, an administrator can only turn the UAC box off or on. In Windows 7, the UAC box can be controlled using the following four options shown in Figure 1-56:

- ◢ Always notify me when programs are trying to install software or make other changes to the computer and when I am making changes to Windows settings. (This is the Vista default option.)
- ◢ Notify me when programs are trying to make changes, but don't notify me when I am changing Windows settings. (This option is new to Windows 7 and causes the UAC box to be less annoying.)
- ◢ Same as the second option above but, in addition, do not dim the Windows desktop. Dimming the Windows desktop can alarm a user and take up resources. (In Vista, a Group Policy setting can be used to disable dimming the desktop.)
- ◢ Never notify me when a program is trying to change the computer or I am changing it. (This option is also available in Vista.)

PERFORMANCE REPORTS AND SETTINGS

Follow these steps to learn how you can use the Action Center tools to view performance reports and adjust Windows for best performance:

1. In the Action Center left pane, click **View performance information** to access tools used to monitor Windows performance. The resulting window (see Figure 1-57) shows

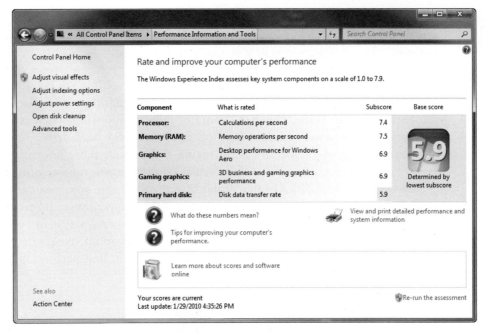

Figure 1-57 The Windows Experience Index gives a rating of key system components
Courtesy: Course Technology/Cengage Learning

the Windows Experience Index that also appears in the Vista System window. The index is used to assess key system components to give a high-level view of the computer's performance. When you click **View and print detailed performance and system information,** more detail appears (see Figure 1-58).

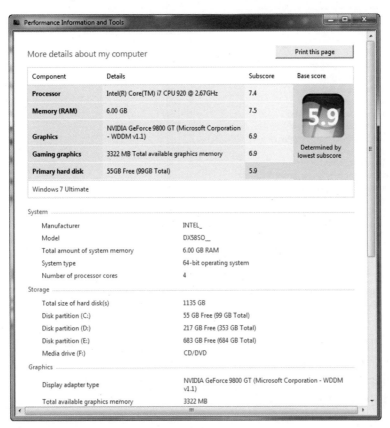

Figure 1-58 Detailed information about key system components
Courtesy: Course Technology/Cengage Learning

A+
220-701
2.5, 3.2,
3.3

Notes The Windows Experience Index is also available in the System window, just as it is in Vista. To access the window, click **Start**, right-click **Computer**, and choose **Properties** from the shortcut menu. The System window works the same way as it does in Vista.

2. Notice the left pane in the Performance and Information and Tools window (refer back to Figure 1-57). This pane contains links to adjusting visual effects, indexing options, and power settings and tools to clean up the hard drive. These utilities can help improve a system's performance and provide more information about the system. For example, click **Adjust visual effects** to open the Performance Options box (see Figure 1-59). On the Visual Effects tab of this box, you can choose to adjust visual effects for best performance or best appearance. If resources are low on a system, adjusting for best performance can remove a system bottleneck hogging resources. You can also enable or disable individual visual effects to customize the visual effects, creating a balance between best performance and best appearance.

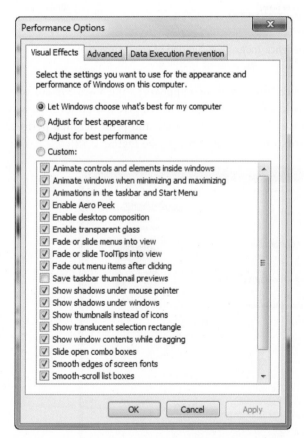

Figure 1-59   Balance visual effects between best performance and best appearance
Courtesy: Course Technology/Cengage Learning

3. Click the **Advanced** tab on the Performance Options box to choose how to allocate processor resources, adjusting for best performance between programs running in the foreground and programs running in the background (see Figure 1-60).

A+
220-701
2.5, 3.2,
3.3

Figure 1-60 Use the Advanced tab of the Performance Options box to adjust how processor resources are allocated to programs and background services
Courtesy: Course Technology/Cengage Learning

4. Also notice on the Advanced tab the ability to adjust virtual memory. Click **Change** to change the size of the paging file or move the file to a different hard drive.

5. Also in the left pane in the Performance and Information and Tools window (refer back to Figure 1-57) you can click **Advanced tools** to access Event Viewer logs and to open Performance Monitor, Resource Monitor, Task Manager, Disk Defragmenter, and other tools.

OTHER TOOLS IN THE ACTION CENTER

Looking back again to the Action Center screen shown in Figure 1-52, notice the links at the bottom of the left pane. Using these links, you can access the Backup and Restore utility, Windows Update, and Windows Program Compatibility Troubleshooter. At the bottom of the right pane in the Action Center, you can open the Windows Troubleshooting utility and the System Restore utility. As you work with Windows 7, you'll learn to appreciate the convenience of the Action Center as a way to easily find tools and perform support tasks.

BACKING UP USER DATA AND THE SYSTEM IMAGE

A+
220-701
2.5

The Windows 7 Backup and Restore utility gives you much more control over what you can choose to back up than does the Vista Backup and Restore utility. In Windows 7, you can choose which user's data to back up and you can also select any folder on the hard drive for backup. In addition, you can back up the Windows 7 volume (called the system image). In this part of the chapter, you will learn how to use the Backup and Restore window and how to create a system image.

WINDOWS 7 BACKUP AND RESTORE

Follow these steps to learn how to use Windows 7 Backup and Restore:

1. To open the Backup and Restore utility, in Control Panel under System and Security, click **Back up your computer**. The first time you open the utility, the window will look like the one in Figure 1-61. Click **Set up backup**.

2. In the next dialog box (see Figure 1-62), select the media to hold the backup. In Figure 1-62, choices in this example are volume E: (a second internal hard drive), the DVD drive, and OneTouch (an external hard drive). Make your selection and click **Next**.

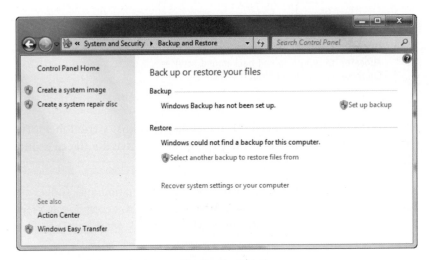

Figure 1-61   Set up a backup routine for the first time
Courtesy: Course Technology/Cengage Learning

> **Notes** Windows 7 Professional, Ultimate, and Enterprise editions allow you to save the backup to a network location. To use a shared folder on the network for the backup destination, click **Save on a network** (Figure 1-62). In the resulting box (see Figure 1-63), click **Browse** and point to the folder. Also enter the user name and password on the remote computer that the backup utility will use to authenticate to that computer when it makes the backup. You cannot save to a network location when using Windows 7 Home editions. For these editions, the button *Save on a network* is missing in the window where you select the backup destination.

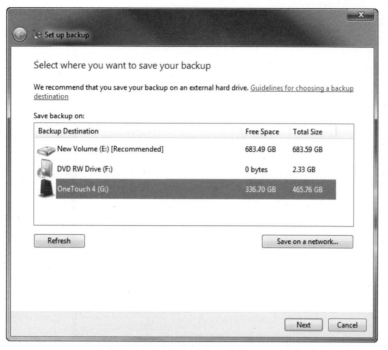

Figure 1-62   Select the destination media to hold the backup
Courtesy: Course Technology/Cengage Learning

Figure 1-63   Select the folder on the network to hold the backup and enter the
username and password for the remote computer
Courtesy: Course Technology/Cengage Learning

3. In the next box (see Figure 1-64), select **Let me choose** so that you can select the
folders to back up. Click **Next**.

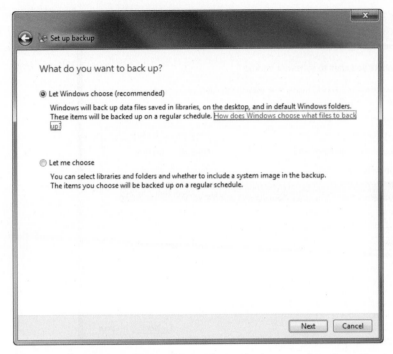

Figure 1-64   Allow Windows to choose what to back up or select the option to choose folders
Courtesy: Course Technology/Cengage Learning

4. In the next box (see Figure 1-65), select the libraries and folders you want to back up. You can click the white triangle beside Local Disk (C:) to drill down to any folder on the hard drive for backup. Check folders or libraries to back up. If the backup media can hold the system image, the option to include the image is selected by default. If you don't want to include the image, uncheck it. Click **Next** to continue.

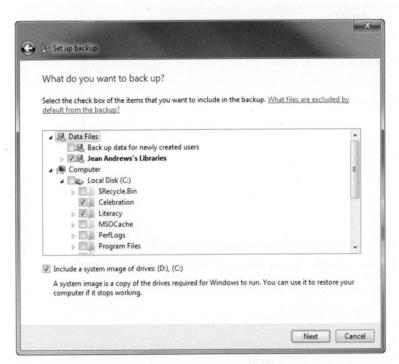

Figure 1-65   Select the folders or libraries to include in the backup
Courtesy: Course Technology/Cengage Learning

1

A+ 220-701

A+
220-701
2.5

5. In the next box, verify the correct folders and libraries are selected (see Figure 1-66). Notice in the figure, the backup is scheduled to run every Sunday at 7:00 PM. To change this schedule, click **Change schedule**. On the next box, you can choose to run the backup daily, weekly, or monthly and select the time of day (see Figure 1-67). Make your selections and click **OK**.

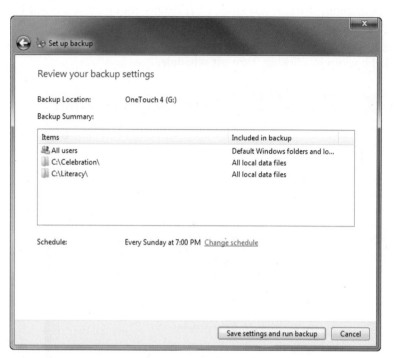

Figure 1-66 Review your backup settings
Courtesy: Course Technology/Cengage Learning

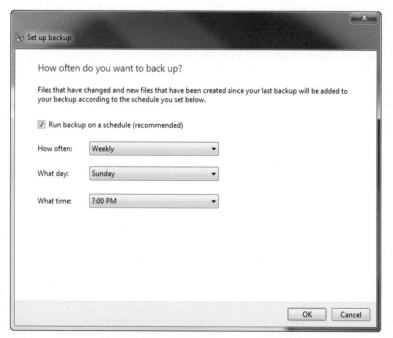

Figure 1-67 Select the backup schedule
Courtesy: Course Technology/Cengage Learning

A+
220-701
2.5

6. Review your backup settings and click **Save settings and run backup** (refer back to Figure 1-66). The backup proceeds. A shadow copy is made of any open files so that files that are currently open are included in the backup.

If you want to later change the settings for your scheduled backup, in Control Panel, open the Backup and Restore window. Notice in Figure 1-68 the window has changed from that shown earlier in Figure 1-61. It now shows the details about the scheduled backup. To change the backup settings, click **Change settings**. Follow the process to verify or change each setting for the backup. Also notice in the left pane of Figure 1-68 that you can turn off the scheduled backup by clicking **Turn off schedule**.

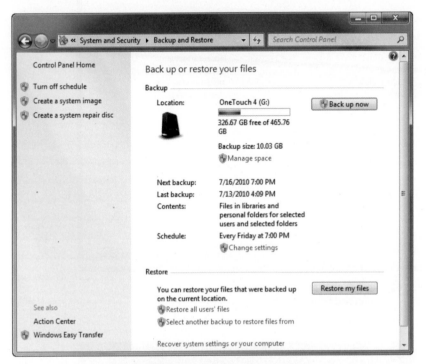

Figure 1-68   View and change backup setting
Courtesy: Course Technology/Cengage Learning

> **Notes** A limitation of Windows 7 Backup and Restore is that you can only have one scheduled backup routine.

If a data file or folder later gets corrupted, you can recover the file or folder using the Backup and Restore window or using the Previous Versions tab of the file or folder Properties box. To use the Backup and Restore window, follow these steps:

1. Make the backup media available to the computer by inserting the backup disc, connecting the external hard drive, or other method.

2. Open the **Backup and Restore** window. Scroll down to the bottom of the window and click **Restore my files**. The Restore Files box appears (see Figure 1-69).

> **Notes** If the *Restore my files* button is missing from the Backup and Restore window, verify the backup media is available to Windows.

A+
220-701
2.5

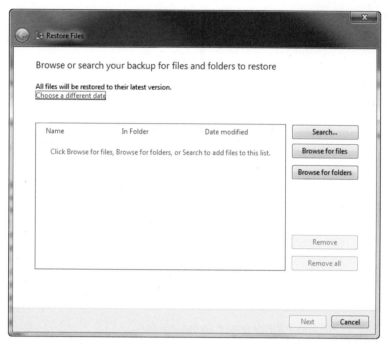

Figure 1-69 Locate the files and folders on the backup media to restore
Courtesy: Course Technology/Cengage Learning

3. Use one of the three buttons on the window to locate the file or folder. *Search* allows you to search for a file or folder when you only know part of the filename or folder name. *Browse for files* allows you to drill down to the file to restore. *Browse for folders* allows you to search for the folder to restore. You can locate and select multiple files or folders to restore. Then click **Next** and follow the directions on-screen to restore all the selected items.

> **Notes** A simple way to open a Windows utility window is to use the *Search programs and files* box. For example, to open the Backup and Restore window, click **Start** and type **Backup** in the box (see Figure 1-70). As you type, programs and files that contain these letters appear. Click the one you want. In the figure, you would click **Backup and Restore.**

A previous version of a file or folder is a version that was previously created by the Backup and Restore utility or by System Protection when it created a restore point for the system. A **restore point** is a snapshot of the Windows system and includes files that have changed since the last restore point was made. To restore a folder or file to a previous version, follow these steps:

1. Copy (do not move) the folder or file to a new location. When you restore a file or folder to a previous version, the current file or folder is lost and replaced by the previous version. By saving a copy of the current file or folder to a different location, you can revert back to the copy if necessary.

2. Right-click the file or folder and select **Restore previous versions** from the shortcut menu. The Properties box for the file or folder appears with the Previous Versions tab selected. Windows displays a list of all previous versions of the file or folder it has kept (see Figure 1-71).

A+
220-701
2.5

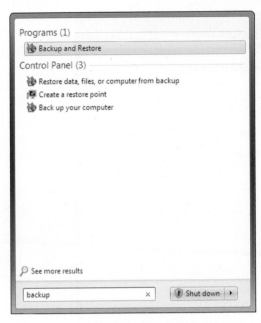

Figure 1-70 Use the Windows 7 search feature to find and open a program or data file
Courtesy: Course Technology/Cengage Learning

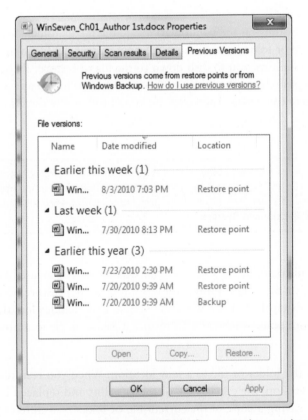

Figure 1-71 Restore a file or folder from a previous version
Courtesy: Course Technology/Cengage Learning

3. Select the version you want and click **Restore.** A message box asks if you are sure you want to continue. Click **Restore** and then click **OK.**

4. Open the restored file or folder and verify it is the version you want. If you decide you need another version, delete the file or folder and copy the file or folder you saved in Step 1 back into the original location. Then return to Step 2 and try again, this time selecting a different previous version.

CREATING A SYSTEM IMAGE

Backup and Restore can be used to create a system image. Here are important points to keep in mind about creating a system image.

- ▲ A system image is a copy of the Windows volume. It includes all system files, user settings, folders, and data on the volume. When you restore a hard drive using the system image, everything on the volume is deleted and replaced with the system image.
- ▲ A system image must always be created on an internal or external hard drive. When using Backup and Restore to back up your files and folders, you can include the system image in the backup procedure. Even if the files and folders are being copied to a USB drive, CD, or DVD, the system image will always be copied to a hard drive.
- ▲ The system image on a hard drive can be found in the path D:\WindowsImageBackup\computer name, where D: is the drive letter of the hard drive receiving the backup and computer name is the name of the computer that is being backed up.
- ▲ In addition to backing up a system image, you should also back up individual folders that contain user data. If individual data files or folders need to be recovered, you cannot rely on the system image because recovering data using the system image would totally replace the entire Windows volume with the system image.

Windows Backup and Restore offers two ways to create a system image:

- ▲ Include backing up the system image as part of the regularly scheduled backup procedure. The system image is backed up to a second hard drive and the image is updated each time the backup is performed according to the backup schedule. How to include the system image in a regularly scheduled backup is covered earlier in the chapter.
- ▲ Create a system image apart from the regularly scheduled backup procedure. To create a system image at any time, in the Backup and Restore window (refer back to Figure 1-68), click **Create a system image** and follow the directions on-screen.

Create a system image any time after Windows is installed, and then you can use this image to recover from a failed hard drive. To use the system image to recover a failed hard drive is called reimaging the drive. The details of how to reimage the drive are covered in Chapter 2.

> **Notes** The system image you create using Backup and Restore can only be installed on the computer that was used to create it. The method used to create a hardware independent system image, called a standard image, is discussed later in the chapter.

Now let's turn our attention to special situations you might encounter when installing and supporting Windows 7 in a large organization.

SPECIAL CONCERNS WHEN WORKING IN A LARGE ENTERPRISE

A+
220-701
3.1, 3.3

Working as a PC support technician in a large corporate environment is different from working as a PC support technician for a small company or with individuals. In this part of the chapter, you will learn how Windows is installed in an enterprise.

DEPLOYMENT STRATEGIES FOR WINDOWS 7

Earlier in the chapter, you learned how to install Windows 7 using the setup DVD or using files downloaded from the Microsoft Web site when a computer does not have a DVD drive. You perform the installation while sitting at the computer, responding to each query made by the setup program. Then you must configure Windows and install device drivers and applications. If, however, you were responsible for installing Windows 7 on several hundred PCs in a large corporation, you might want a less time-consuming method to perform the installations. These methods are called deployment strategies. A deployment strategy is a procedure to install Windows, device drivers, and applications on a computer and can include the process to transfer user settings, application settings, and user data files from an old installation to the new installation.

Microsoft suggests four deployment strategies; the one chosen depends on the number of computers to be deployed and determines the amount of time you must sit in front of an individual computer as Windows is installed on it (this time is called the touch time). As a PC support technician in a large corporation, most likely you would not be involved in choosing or setting up the deployment strategy. But you need to be aware of the different strategies so that you have a general idea of what will be expected of you when you are asked to provide desk-side or help-desk support as Windows is being deployed in your organization.

The four deployment strategies are discussed next.

HIGH-TOUCH WITH RETAIL MEDIA (RECOMMENDED FOR FEWER THAN 100 COMPUTERS)

The high-touch with retail media strategy is the strategy used in the installations described earlier in the chapter. Except for upgrade installations, applications must be manually installed after the OS is installed. To transfer user settings, application settings, and user data files to a new installation, you can use Windows Easy Transfer (a manual process that is easy to use) or the User State Migration Tool (more automated and more difficult to set up and use). Windows Easy Transfer is part of Windows 7. The User State Migration Tool (USMT) is included in the Windows Automated Installation Kit (AIK) that can be downloaded from the Microsoft Web site. The kit contains the software tools and documentation needed to set up high-volume deployments of Windows and applications.

HIGH-TOUCH WITH STANDARD IMAGE (RECOMMENDED FOR 100 TO 200 COMPUTERS)

To use the high-touch with standard image strategy, a system administrator prepares an image, called a standard image, that includes Windows 7, drivers, and applications. The image is created using tools included in the Windows AIK. The image is usually stored on an 8 GB or larger bootable USB flash drive. A technician starts the installation manually by booting from this flash drive. This one installation process installs Windows, all device drivers, and applications. USMT can be used to transfer user settings and user data files to the new installation.

A+
220-701
3.1, 3.3

This strategy takes longer to set up than the previous strategy because a system administrator must prepare the image and must set up USMT, but it takes less time to install on each computer and also assures the administrator that each computer has a standard set of applications and is configured correctly.

> **Notes** If you're interested in learning how to create a standard image that is hardware independent, check out this video at the Microsoft Technet site: *technet.microsoft.com/en-us/windows/ee530017.aspx*. For a detailed step-by-step guide to create a standard image, go to this link: *technet.microsoft.com/en-us/library/ee523217(WS.10).aspx*.

LITE-TOUCH, HIGH-VOLUME DEPLOYMENT (RECOMMENDED FOR 200 TO 500 COMPUTERS)

The lite-touch, high-volume deployment strategy uses a deployment server on the network to serve up the installation after a technician starts the process. The files in the installation include Windows, device drivers, and applications, and collectively are called the distribution share.

The technician starts the installation by booting the computer to Windows PE. Windows Preinstallation Environment (Windows PE) is a minimum operating system used to start the installation. It can be installed on a USB flash drive or CD to make the device bootable and is included in the Windows AIK. The technician boots from the device, which might be configured to display a menu to choose from multiple distribution shares available on the deployment server. The technician can also boot the PC directly to the network to receive Windows PE from the deployment server. To boot to the network, use BIOS setup to set the first item in the boot device priority to be Ethernet (see Figure 1-72). Then reboot the system. The system boots to the Preboot eXecution Environment (PXE), also known as the Pre-Execution Environment. PXE searches for a server on the network to provide a bootable OS (Windows PE).

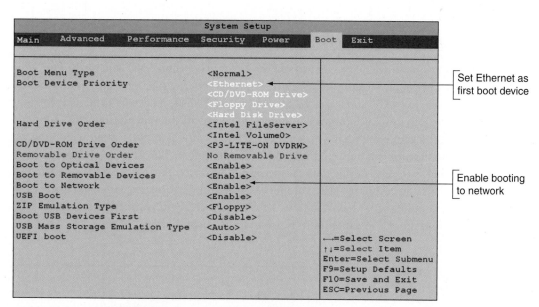

Figure 1-72 Configure BIOS setup to boot to the network
Courtesy: Course Technology/Cengage Learning

After the installation begins, the technician is not required to respond to prompts by the setup program. These responses, such as the administrator password or domain name, are stored in an answer file. The User State Migration Tool is used to transfer user settings and user data files to the new installation.

For high-touch strategies, a technician would normally sit at a computer and use the Windows 7 Upgrade Advisor to determine if the system qualifies for Windows 7 before Windows 7 is installed. Using lite-touch deployments, a more automated method of qualifying a computer is preferred. The Microsoft Assessment and Planning (MAP) Toolkit can be used by a system administrator from a network location to query hundreds of computers in a single scan. The software automatically examines hardware and applications on each computer to verify compatibility with Windows 7. The MAP software might also be used by the system administrator before deciding to deploy a new OS to determine what computer hardware upgrades or application software upgrades are required that must be included in the overall deployment budget.

ZERO-TOUCH, HIGH-VOLUME DEPLOYMENT (RECOMMENDED FOR MORE THAN 500 COMPUTERS)

The zero-touch, high-volume deployment strategy is the most difficult to set up and requires complex tools. The installation does not require the user to start the process (called pull automation). Rather, the installation uses push automation, meaning that a server automatically pushes the installation to a computer when a user is not likely to be sitting at it. The entire installation is automated and no user intervention is required. The process can turn on a computer that is turned off and even works when no OS is installed on the computer or the current OS is corrupted.

> **Notes** PC support technicians find that large enterprises appreciate quick and easy solutions to desktop or laptop computer problems. Technicians quickly learn their marching orders are almost always "replace or reimage." Little time is given to trying to solve the underlying problem when hardware can quickly be replaced or a Windows installation can quickly be reimaged.

USING THE USMT SOFTWARE

Let's look briefly at what to expect when using the USMT software. The Windows 7 version of USMT is version 4.0, is much improved over earlier versions, and is included in the Windows AIK software. To prepare to use USMT, a system administrator must first install the AIK software on his computer. In Microsoft documentation, this computer is called the technician computer. The source computer is the computer from which the user settings, application settings, and user data files are taken. The destination computer is the computer that is to receive this data. Sometimes the source computer and the destination computer are the same computer. An example is when you perform a clean installation of Windows 7 on a computer that has Windows XP installed and you want to transfer user files and settings from the XP installation to the Windows 7 installation.

> **Notes** USMT 4.0 is the first version of USMT to use hard-link migration of user files and settings designed to be used when the source and destination computers are the same computer. Hard-link migration does not actually copy files and settings, but leaves them on the hard drive without copying. This method makes USMT extremely fast when the hard drive is not formatted during the Windows installation.

The USMT software uses two commands: ScanState migrates settings and files from the source computer to a safe location, and LoadState applies these settings and files to the destination computer. Here are the general steps to use USMT:

1. Download and install the AIK software on the technician computer.

2. Copy the USMT program files from the technician computer to the source computer.

3. Run the ScanState command on the source computer to copy user files and settings to a file server or other safe location.

4. Install Windows 7, device drivers, and applications on the destination computer.

5. Run the LoadState command to apply user files and settings from the file server to the destination computer.

The details of the parameters for the ScanState and LoadState commands are not covered in this book. Ask the system administrator responsible for setting up USMT for the specific command lines used by your organization.

> **Notes** For detailed instructions on using USMT that a system administrator might use, go to *technet.microsoft.com* and search on "using USMT for IT professionals."

WHAT TO EXPECT WHEN USING IPV6

Many enterprise organizations are converting from IPv4 to IPv6. In addition, a portion of the Internet has already converted to IPv6. As a technician in an enterprise, you need to be aware of how IP addresses using IPv6 are read and how to support this standard.

An IP address is a series of numbers that uniquely identifies a node on a TCP/IP network including the Internet and an intranet. The standard that determines an IP address with 32 bits is called the IPv4 (Internet Protocol version 4) standard. Partly because of potential shortages of IP addresses and partly because of the need for increased security on the Internet, the IPv6 (IP version 6) standard has been introduced. IPv6 uses 128 bits for an IP address. All versions of Windows since Windows XP with Service Pack 2 support IPv6.

Let's first look at IPv6 terminology and addressing and then at how Windows 7 uses IPv6.

IPV6 TERMINOLOGY

Here are a few facts about writing and displaying IPv6 addresses:

◢ An IPv6 address has 128 bits that are written as 8 blocks of hexadecimal numbers separated by colons, like this: 2001:0000:0B80:0000:0000:00D3:9C5A:00CC.

◢ Each block is 16 bits. For example, the first block in the address above is 2001 in hex, which can be written as 0010 0000 0000 0001 in binary.

◢ Leading zeros in a 4-character hex block can be eliminated. For example, the IP address above can be written as 2001:0000:B80:0000:0000:D3:9C5A:CC.

◢ If blocks contain all zeroes, they can be written as double colons (::). The IP address above can be written two ways:

• 2001::B80:0000:0000:D3:9C5A:CC

• 2001:0000:B80::D3:9C5A:CC

To avoid confusion, only one set of double colons is used in an IP address. In this example, the preferred method is the second one: 2001:0000:B80::D3:9C5A:CC

Here are a few terms used in the IPv6 standards:

▲ A link, sometimes called the local link, is a local area network (LAN) or wide area network (WAN) bounded by routers.

▲ A subnet is one or more links that have the same 64 bits in the first part of the IP address (called the prefix). Recall that when using IPv4, the subnet could be identified by any number of bits at the beginning of the IP address. Using IPv6, the subnet is almost always identified using the first 64 bits.

> **? To Learn More**   To learn more about subnets and subnet masks, see pages 881 through 882 in Chapter 17 of *A+ Guide to Managing and Maintaining Your PC,* 7th edition, or pages 389 through 390 in Chapter 8 of *A+ Guide to Software,* 5th edition.

▲ Neighbors are two or more nodes on the same link.

▲ An interface is a node's attachment to a link. The attachment can be a physical attachment using a network adapter or wireless connection or a logical attachment such as when a tunneling protocol is used to connect the node to a server.

▲ The last 64 bits or 4 blocks of an IP address identify the interface and are called the interface ID or interface identifier. These 64 bits uniquely identify an interface on the local link.

IPv6 does not use classes of addresses as does IPv4. Instead it supports these three types of IP addresses:

▲ Using a unicast address, packets are delivered to a single node on a network.

▲ Using a multicast address, packets are delivered to all nodes on a network.

▲ An anycast address is used by routers. The address identifies multiple destinations and packets are delivered to the closest destination.

A unicast address identifies a single interface on a network. Three types of unicast addresses are:

▲ A global unicast address can be routed on the Internet. These addresses are similar to IPv4 public IP addresses.

▲ A link-local unicast address can be used for communicating with nodes in the same link. These addresses are similar to IPv4 private IP addresses and are sometimes called link-local addresses.

▲ A unique local unicast address can work on multiple links within the same organization. The address is a hybrid between a global unicast address that works on the Internet and a link-local unicast address that works on only one link.

Table 1-5 shows the currently used address prefixes for these types of IP addresses. In the future, we can expect more prefixes to be assigned as they are needed.

IP Address Type	Address Prefix
Global unicast	2000::
Link-local unicast	FE80::
Unique local unicast	FC00:: and FD00::
Multicast	FF00::

Table 1-5   Address prefixes for types of IPv6 addresses

A+
220-701
4.1

WINDOWS 7 SUPPORT FOR IPV6

Windows 7 supports both IPv4 and IPv6 on the same network and both standards are enabled by default. To see how Windows 7 assigns IP addresses to a computer, consider an example using the ipconfig command shown in Figure 1-73.

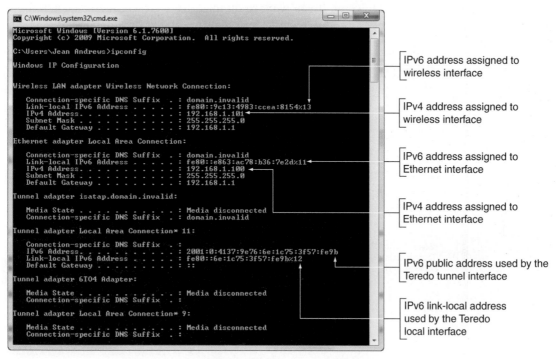

Figure 1-73   The ipconfig command showing IPv4 and IPv6 addresses assigned to this computer
            Courtesy: Course Technology/Cengage Learning

Notice in the figure the four IP addresses that have been assigned to the physical connections:

- Windows has assigned the wireless connection two IP addresses, one using IPv4 and one using IPv6.
- The Ethernet LAN connection has also been assigned an IPv4 address and an IPv6 address.

The IPv6 addresses are followed by a % sign and a number; for example, %13 follows the first IP address. This number is called the zone ID or scope ID and is used to identify the interface in a list of interfaces for this computer.

Also notice in the figure the information given about tunnels. A tunnel is a passageway through or under something. Tunnels are used by IPv6 to transport IPv6 packets through or over an IPv4 network. Three tunneling protocols have been developed to do this:

- ISATAP (pronounced "eye-sa-tap") stands for Intra-Site Automatic Tunnel Addressing Protocol).
- Teredo (pronounced "ter-EE-do") is named after the Teredo worm that bores holes in wood. IPv6 addresses intended to be used by this protocol begin with 2001::.
- 6TO4, also called 6over4, is an older tunneling protocol being replaced by the more powerful Teredo or ISATAP protocols.

The local network does not have a DHCP server serving up IPv6 addresses. (This missing server would have been called a DHCPv6 server.) Therefore, the IPv6 addresses

A+
220-701
4.1

were automatically assigned by Windows to each physical interface using a process called address autoconfiguration. When an interface is a physical interface, such as one made by an Ethernet adapter, the MAC address of the adapter is used to generate the last 64-bits of the IP address, which is called the interface ID.

In most situations, you can simply leave TCP/IP settings at default values to enable both IPv4 and IPv6. However, if you want to disable IPv6 for each physical connection, use the connection's Properties box. Follow these steps to disable IPv6 for the local area connection:

1. In the Network and Sharing Center, click **Local Area Connection**. The connection status box appears. Notice in Figure 1-74 that IPv4 shows Internet connectivity but IPv6 does not.

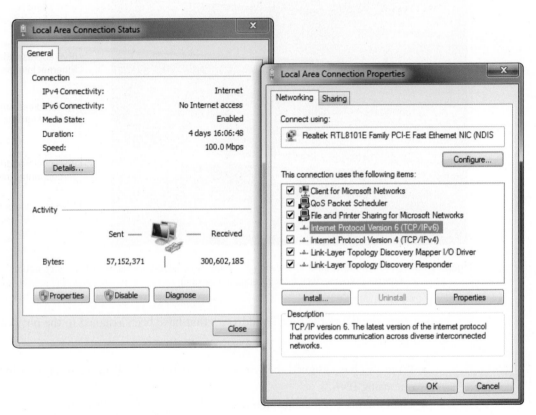

Figure 1-74 Enable or disable the TCP/IPv6 protocol
Courtesy: Course Technology/Cengage Learning

2. Click **Properties**. In the Properties box, uncheck **Internet Protocol Version 6 (TCP/IPv6)**.

3. Click **OK** and **Close** to close the two boxes.

>> **CHAPTER SUMMARY**

◢ Windows 7 performs better than Vista and uses fewer resources. Support tools available in Windows 7 are fundamentally the same as those in Vista although names and the way they are accessed sometimes differ.

◢ The Windows 7 taskbar is designed to provide a Jump List when you right-click an open program's icon in the taskbar. The rectangle on the far right of the taskbar can use Aero Peek to control open windows.

◢ Windows 7 has Windows Touch that supports a multi-touch screen.

◢ Aero Snap and Aero Shake can be used to maximize, minimize, and resize windows.

◢ A library is a collection of folders and their contents. These files and other folders can be located in any storage media on the local computer or on the network. A library is a convenient way to access several folders in different locations from one central location.

◢ Windows XP Mode allows you to run older applications that are not compatible with Windows 7. The Windows XP Mode software runs in a Windows Virtual PC environment.

◢ The Action Center is a centralized location that alerts the user to issues that might need addressing and provides centralized access to many Windows 7 support tools.

◢ A homegroup works like a workgroup in Vista and XP, but is easier to set up and uses a homegroup password. It does not require that users have a user account and password on a remote computer to access resources on that computer from the network.

◢ Windows Live Essentials includes free programs you can download and use in Windows 7. Microsoft Security Essentials is free antivirus software.

◢ Editions of Windows 7 are Windows 7 Starter, Home Basic, Home Premium, Professional, Enterprise, and Ultimate.

◢ All editions of Windows 7 except the Starter edition can be purchased using 32-bit or 64-bit code. The retail version of Windows 7 comes with two DVDs: a 32-bit DVD and a 64-bit DVD.

◢ A 32-bit OS cannot address as much RAM as a 64-bit OS. The ability to use more RAM is one reason to use a 64-bit OS.

◢ Before purchasing Windows 7, make sure your system meets the recommended hardware requirements and all the hardware and applications will work under the OS.

◢ The Windows 7 Upgrade Advisor is software that can be downloaded and run on a computer to determine if it qualifies for Windows 7.

◢ You can purchase the less expensive upgrade license of Windows 7 if you already have a license for Windows XP or Vista for your computer.

◢ If you are upgrading Windows XP to Windows 7, you must perform a custom or clean install.

◢ Some editions of Windows Vista can be upgraded to Windows 7, bringing forward into the new installation user settings and installed applications. The process is called an in-place upgrade.

◢ You can start a Windows installation by booting from a DVD, USB drive, or other boot media. You can also install the OS from files stored on another computer on the network.

◢ Windows can be installed as an in-place upgrade, a clean installation, or in a dual-boot environment with another OS.

◢ To use an upgrade license of Windows 7 on a new hard drive, you can install Windows 7 twice. The first time do not enter the product key. Then on the second installation, enter the product key and activate the OS.

◢ After the installation, affix the OEM product key sticker to the computer, verify that you have network access, activate Windows, install updates and service packs for Windows, verify automatic updates are set as you want them, install hardware, install applications, and turn Windows features on or off.

◢ If you have problems connecting to a network, check for solutions in the Network and Sharing Center, verify homegroup and network discovery settings, and consider that you might need to join a corporate domain.

◢ If you have problems with installing legacy hardware devices or applications, consider using Windows 7 compatibility mode.

◢ If legacy applications don't work in compatibility mode, consider using Windows XP Mode.

◢ Information available in the Action Center includes current problems and suggested Windows 7 solutions. In the Action Center, you can also view and change security and maintenance settings. You can also view performance reports and change settings to improve performance. Recovery, backup, and troubleshooting tools are also available in the Action Center.

◢ Backup and Restore can be used to back up user data, specified folders, and the system image. Only one backup can be scheduled. Using Windows 7 Professional, Ultimate, or Enterprise editions, you can back up to a network location.

◢ A Windows 7 system image can only be saved to an internal or external local or network hard drive.

◢ Microsoft recommends four different deployment strategies for Windows 7 depending on how many computers are to be deployed. The four strategies are (a) high-touch with retail media, (b) high-touch with a standard image, (c) lite-touch, high-volume deployment, and (d) zero-touch, high-volume deployment.

◢ The User State Migration Tool (USMT) can be used to transfer user and application settings and user data files from the old Windows installation to the new one.

◢ High-touch deployment strategies use a standard image that is hardware independent and contains Windows, device drivers, and applications.

◢ Lite-touch and zero-touch high-volume deployment strategies use a distribution share stored on a file server.

◢ Lite-touch, high-volume deployment uses Windows PE to boot the PC. Windows PE can be loaded from a bootable removable media or from the deployment server using the PC's Preboot eXecution Environment (PXE).

◢ The Microsoft Assessment and Planning (MAP) Toolkit is used to automatically scan multiple computers on a network to verify that each computer and its applications qualify for Windows 7.

◢ When using USMT, first use the ScanState command to create the migration store before you install Windows. After the Windows installation, use the LoadState command to apply the store to the new installation.

◢ IPv6 uses 128-bit IP addresses. The addresses are written in 8 blocks of hexadecimal numbers.

◢ Three tunneling protocols used to transition from IPv4 to IPv6 are ISATAP, Teredo, and 6TO4, which send IPv6 packets over an IPv4 network.

◢ By default, Windows 7 enables both IPv4 and IPv6 protocols.

>> KEY TERMS

6over4 – *See* 6TO4.

6TO4 – An older tunneling protocol used by IPv6 to transport IPv6 packets through or over an IPv4 network. It is being replaced by the more powerful Teredo or ISATAP protocols. *Also called* 6over4.

Action Center – A window that brings together many Windows utilities and reporting features to provide information about the system and to solve problems that Windows is aware of and can offer a possible solution.

Aero Peek – A Windows 7 feature that allows you to view the desktop when you mouse over the small rectangle to the right of the taskbar, causing all open windows to become transparent. Click the rectangle to minimize all open windows.

Aero Shake – A Windows 7 feature that causes all windows to minimize except the window you are shaking. To shake a window, click your mouse in the title bar of the window and drag it back and forth quickly.

Aero Snap – A Windows feature that causes a window to fill the right or left side of your screen when you drag the window to the far right or far left side, respectively. Dragging a window to the top of the screen causes the window to maximize. Dragging a window that is maximized downward causes it to restore to its original size before it was maximized.

answer file – A file that contains all answers that the Windows setup process prompts the user to enter during the installation.

anycast address – Using IPv6, an IP address assigned to multiple routers, usually in the same network. A packet is delivered to the closest router among the routers assigned this IP address.

boot loader menu – A startup menu that gives the user the choice of which operating system to load, such as Windows 7 or Windows Vista, which are both installed on the same system, creating a dual boot.

Certificate of Authenticity – A sticker that includes the Windows product key to be pasted on the exterior of a new computer when Windows is installed using an OEM (Original Equipment Manufacturer) version of the OS.

clean install – A Windows installation that creates a fresh installation of Windows and does not carry forward user settings or installed applications. The Windows 7 setup program calls this type of installation a custom installation.

compatibility mode – A group of settings that can be applied to older drivers or applications that might cause them to work in Windows 7.

custom installation – *See* clean install.

deployment strategy – A procedure to install Windows, device drivers, and applications on a computer and can include the process to transfer user settings, application settings, and user data files from an old installation to the new installation. The strategy used depends on the number of computers to deploy.

distribution share – The Windows installation files stored on a file server to be deployed using a lite-touch or zero-touch deployment strategy. After the installation is begun, no user interaction is required.

dual boot – The ability to boot using either of two different OSs, such as Windows 7 and Windows Vista.

global unicast address – An IPv6 address that can be routed on the Internet. These addresses are similar to IPv4 public IP addresses.

high-touch with retail media – A deployment strategy requiring manually installing Windows, device drivers, and applications that is used when the number of computers to deploy is fewer than 100.

high-touch with standard image – A deployment strategy recommended when the number of computers to deploy is 100 to 200 that require a standard image of Windows 7, which can include drivers and applications. The image is created using tools included in the Windows Automated Installation Kit (AIK). A technician starts the installation manually by booting from a bootable device, such as a bootable USB flash drive, that holds the image.

homegroup – In Windows 7, a logical group of computers in which resources are shared on a local network. All computers must use the same homegroup password. Specific files, folders, libraries, and printers are shared to the homegroup by the computer. Any user on a remote computer can access resources shared to the homegroup by other computers.

in-place upgrade – A Windows installation that is launched from the Windows desktop and the installation carries forward user settings and installed applications from the old OS to the new one. A Windows OS is already *in place* before you begin the new installation.

interface – Using IPv6, a node's attachment to a link. The attachment can be a physical attachment using a network adapter or wireless connection or a logical attachment such as when a tunneling protocol is used to connect the node to a server.

interface ID – Using IPv6, the last 64 bits of an IP address that uniquely identify an interface on the local link. *Also called* the interface identifier.

ISATAP – Stands for Intra-Site Automatic Tunnel Addressing Protocol and pronounced "eye-sa-tap," a tunneling protocol used by IPv6 to transport IPv6 packets through or over an IPv4 network.

Jump List – A list of major functions available from an application when you right-click the icon of the open application in the Windows 7 taskbar.

library – A collection of folders and their contents, which can physically be located on any media the computer can access. One folder in the library is designated the default save location. When a file is added to the library, it is stored in this folder. When a folder is added to the library, it remains at its original location and is listed in the library.

link – Using IPv6, a local area network (LAN) or wide area network (WAN) bounded by routers. *Also called* the local link.

link-local unicast address – An IPv6 address that can be used for communicating with nodes in the same link. These addresses are similar to IPv4 private IP addresses.

lite-touch high-volume deployment – A deployment strategy that uses a server on the network to serve up the installation, called the distribution share. A technician sitting at the computer starts the installation, but no further manual involvement is required.

local link – *See* link.

Microsoft Assessment and Planning (MAP) Toolkit – Software that is used before Windows 7 is deployed to verify that hardware and applications on multiple computers qualify for Windows 7.

Microsoft Security Essentials – Antivirus software that can be downloaded for free from the Microsoft Web site at *www.microsoft.com/security_essentials*.

multicast address – An IPv6 address that is delivered to all nodes on a network.

multi-touch – A function of some touch screens that allows a user to use two fingers to zoom in or out on the screen.

neighbors – Using IPv6, two or more nodes on the same link.

Preboot eXecution Environment or **Pre-Execution Environment (PXE)** – BIOS firmware that can be used at startup to locate a server on the network to provide Windows PE.

pull automation – An installation strategy that requires a user at the computer to start the installation.

push automation – An installation strategy in which a server automatically pushes the installation to a computer when a user is not likely to be sitting at it.

restore point – A snapshot of the Windows system, usually made before installation of new hardware or applications.

shadow copy – A copy of an open file that is made so that the file can be included in the backup that is currently in progress.

standard image – A hardware-independent image of a Windows installation that can include drivers and applications, created using Windows AIK tools.

subnet – Using IPv6, one or more links that have the same 64 bits in the first part of the IP address (called the prefix).

system image – A backup of the entire Windows volume which can be used to restore the entire Windows system to its condition when the backup was made.

Teredo – Pronounced "ter-EE-do," a tunneling protocol used by IPv6 to transport IPv6 packets through or over an IPv4 network. IPv6 addresses intended to be used by this protocol begin with 2001::.

unicast address – An IPv6 address that is destined for a single node on a network.

unique local unicast address – An IPv6 address that can work on multiple links within the same organization. The address is a hybrid between a global unicast address that works on the Internet and a link-local unicast address that works on only one link.

User State Migration Tool (USMT) – Software used to transfer user settings, application settings, and user data files from the old Windows installation to the new installation.

Windows 7 Enterprise – A Windows 7 edition intended for corporate use, available with multiple site licensing, and which includes BitLocker Drive Encryption.

Windows 7 Home Basic – A Windows 7 edition designed for low-cost home computers that don't require full security or networking features. The edition does not include multimedia utilities, including Windows DVD Maker and the Windows Media Center.

Windows 7 Home Premium – A Windows 7 edition designed for home or small office use where computers are secured by a peer-to-peer network and cannot join a domain. The edition includes multimedia utilities such as Windows DVD Maker and Windows Media Center, but does not include advanced security features such as the Encrypted File System or BitLocker Drive Encryption.

Windows 7 Professional – A Windows 7 edition designed for business use and which includes the ability to join a domain and support for Group Policy and the Encrypted File System. Multiple site licensing is available with this edition. The edition does not include BitLocker Drive Encryption.

Windows 7 Starter – The most limited Windows 7 edition intended for developing nations and use on netbooks. It is the only edition that does not include a 64-bit version.

Windows 7 Ultimate – A Windows 7 edition that includes all features available on all other editions. Multiple licensing is not available.

Windows Live Essentials – Programs that can be downloaded for free from the Microsoft Web site at *www.live.com* and include Messenger, Photo Gallery, Mail, Writer, Movie Maker, Family Safety, and Toolbar.

Windows Preinstallation Environment (Windows PE) – A minimum operating system used to start the Windows installation and is one software tool available in the Windows Automated Installation Kit (AIK).

Windows Touch – A Windows 7 feature that supports touch screens and includes support for multi-touch.

Windows XP Mode – A virtual operating system environment available for Windows 7 that is installed in a virtual PC and allows you to run older applications that are not compatible with Windows 7. Windows XP Mode and Windows Virtual PC are downloaded for free from the Microsoft Web site at this link: *www.microsoft.com/windows/virtual-pc/support.*

zero-touch, high-volume deployment – The most difficult deployment strategy to set up, requiring complex tools. The installation is pushed to the computer from a server, requires no manual interaction, and is recommended when the number of computers to deploy is more than 500.

>> REVIEWING THE BASICS

1. When you move a file into the Windows 7 Documents library, what is the default folder in which the file is stored, assuming the default folder has not been changed from the original Windows setting?

2. What two folders are included by default in the Documents library?

3. What Windows 7 tool replaces the Vista Security Center?

4. By default, Windows Mail is not included in Windows 7. What Microsoft Web site offers Windows Mail as a free download to your Windows 7 PC?

5. What is the name of the free Microsoft antivirus software that can be used with Windows 7?

6. Which Windows 7 edition does not have a 64-bit version?

7. Which three Windows 7 editions can be used to join a domain?

8. What is the maximum amount of RAM that 32-bit Windows 7 Ultimate can address?

9. What is the maximum amount of RAM that 64-bit Windows 7 Home Premium can address?

10. What is the recommended amount of RAM needed to run a 32-bit Windows 7 installation?

11. How much space on the hard drive does it take to install a 32-bit version of Windows 7?

12. Can you perform an in-place upgrade installation of Windows XP Professional to Windows 7 Professional?

13. Can you use the upgrade DVD of Windows 7 Home Premium to perform a clean install on a PC that already has Windows XP Professional installed?

14. What does the Windows 7 setup program call a clean install?

15. Can you perform an in-place upgrade of Vista Ultimate to Windows 7 Home Premium?

16. If you are trying to set up a dual boot between Windows 7 and Windows Vista on a computer with only one hard drive, what is the minimum number of partitions this drive must have?

17. Can you perform an in-place upgrade of Windows 7 by booting from the Windows 7 setup DVD?

18. What Windows 7 or Vista tool can be used to shrink or extend the size of a partition?

19. Are you required to enter the product key during the Windows 7 installation?

20. After a Windows installation, what is the easiest way to determine that you have Internet access?

21. How many days do you have after a Windows 7 installation to activate the OS?

22. You have just upgraded your system to Windows 7. What are three steps you can take when a legacy application does not install in Windows 7?

23. What does Windows 7 call a backup of the entire Windows 7 volume?

24. What tool is represented by the flag icon in the Windows 7 taskbar?

25. Which editions of Windows 7 allow you to save a scheduled backup to a network location?

26. What is the software a system administrator would use to determine if 300 computers in an enterprise qualify for Windows 7?

27. When installing Windows and transferring user data to the new installation, which of these three functions should be performed first? (a) install Windows, (b) use ScanState, or (c) use LoadState

28. How many bits are in an IP address that follows the IPv6 standard?

29. How many bits are normally used to identify the subnet in an IPv6 address?

30. What are the first four hex characters in an IP address using IPv6 that can be used on the Internet?

>> THINKING CRITICALLY

1. You are planning an upgrade from Windows Vista to Windows 7. Your system uses a network card that you don't find listed on the Microsoft Windows 7 list of compatible devices. What do you do next?

   a. Abandon the upgrade and continue to use Windows Vista.

   b. Check the Web site of the NIC manufacturer for a Windows 7 driver.

c. Buy a new network card.

d. Install a dual boot for Windows 7 and Windows Vista and only use the network when you have Windows Vista loaded.

2. You have just installed Windows 7 and now attempt to install your favorite game that worked fine under Windows XP. When you attempt the installation, you get an error. What is your best next step?

a. Purchase a new version of your game, one that is compatible with Windows 7.

b. Download any service packs or patches to Windows 7.

c. Reinstall Windows XP.

3. If you find out that one of your applications is not supported by Windows 7 and you still want to use Windows 7, what can you do to solve this incompatibility problem?

4. Is it possible to install Windows 7 on a system that does not have a DVD drive? Explain your answer.

5. You want to set up two backup schedules for a Windows 7 system, one to back up the system image weekly and the other to back up the \Users folder daily. What is your best approach?

a. Create two backup schedules using the Windows 7 Backup and Restore window, one to run daily and the other to run weekly.

b. Create one backup schedule using the Windows 7 Backup and Restore window and another backup schedule using third-party backup software.

c. It is not possible to set up two backup schedules on the same computer. You must back up both the \Users folder and the system image daily using a single backup schedule.

d. Create one backup schedule using the Windows 7 Backup and Restore window to back up the system image. It is not necessary to also back up the \Users folder because it is included in the system image.

6. You use the ipconfig command to view the IP addresses assigned to a computer and notice two of the IP addresses are 2001:0:4137:9e76:6e:1c75:3f57:fe9b and fe80::6e:1c75:3f57:fe9b. Which of the statements below can you conclude from your observations?

a. IPv6 has been disabled on this computer.

b. The two IP addresses are assigned to the same interface because they are assigned to the same computer.

c. The two IP addresses are assigned to an ISATAP tunnel interface.

d. The two IP addresses are assigned to the same interface because the last 64 bits match.

>> HANDS-ON PROJECTS

PROJECT 1-1: Preparing for Windows 7

Use the Windows 7 Compatibility Center at *www.microsoft.com/windows/compatibility/windows-7/en-us/default.aspx* to research whether a home or lab PC that does not have Windows 7 installed qualifies for Windows 7. Fill in the following table and print the Web pages showing whether each hardware device and application installed on the PC qualifies for Windows 7.

Hardware Device or Application	Specific Device Name or Application Name and Version	Does It Qualify for Windows 7?
Motherboard or BIOS		
Video card		
Modem card (if present)		
Sound card (if present)		
Printer (if present)		
Network card (if present)		
CD-ROM drive (if present)		
DVD drive (if present)		
SCSI hard drive (if present)		
Other device		
Application 1		
Application 2		
Application 3		

PROJECT 1-2:   Preparing for an Upgrade

On a PC with Windows Vista or XP installed, access the Microsoft Web site (*www.microsoft.com*) and locate and run the Windows 7 Upgrade Advisor to find out if the PC is ready for a Windows 7 installation. Make a list of any hardware or software components found incompatible with Windows 7, and draw up a plan for getting the system ready for a Windows 7 upgrade.

PROJECT 1-3:   Updating Windows

On a Windows 7 system connected to the Internet, click **Start, All Programs,** and **Windows Update.** This takes you to the Microsoft Web site, which searches your system and recommends Windows updates. Print the Web page showing a list of recommended updates. For a lab PC, don't perform the updates unless you have your instructor's permission.

PROJECT 1-4:   Installing and Running Microsoft Virtual PC

On a Windows XP or Vista computer, go to the Microsoft Web site (*www.microsoft.com*) and download Virtual PC. Install Virtual PC on your computer. Use it to install a 32-bit version of Windows 7. (Virtual PC does not support a 64-bit OS.) You do not have to activate the OS and you will have 30 days to use it before it will not work. You can use the installation in the next 30 days as you work through the projects and labs using Windows 7 in this book.

PROJECT 1-5:   Using the Action Center

Using Windows 7, follow these steps to use the Action Center:

1. Open the Action Center and list any problems it reports.

2. Apply any solutions not yet applied. Make notes regarding the solutions you applied and the results of applying these solutions.

3. List any problems that are still not resolved.

4. For each unresolved problem, suggest other solutions than the ones the Action Center gives.

PROJECT 1-6: Using the Internet for Problem Solving

Access the *support.microsoft.com* Web site for Windows 7 support. Print one article from the Knowledge Base that addresses a problem when installing Windows 7.

PROJECT 1-7: Installing Windows 7

Follow the instructions in the chapter to install Windows 7 as either an upgrade or clean install. Write down each decision you had to make as you performed the installation. If you get any error messages during the installation, write them down and list the steps you took to recover from the error. How long did the installation take?

PROJECT 1-8: Investigating the Windows Automated Installation Kit (AIK)

The Windows Automated Installation Kit (AIK) is a group of tools and documentation that IT professionals can use to deploy Windows and can be downloaded for free from the Microsoft Web site. Here are the tools included in the AIK:

◢ User State Migration Tool (USMT) that you learned about in this chapter

◢ ImageX, used to create and modify standard images

◢ Deployment Image Servicing and Management (DISM), used to apply updates, drivers, and language packs to an existing Windows image

◢ Windows System Image Manager (SIM), used to create answer files and manage distribution shares and images

◢ Windows Preinstallation Environment (Windows PE), the minimal operating system that is used to install Windows. Place it on a DVD, USB flash drive, or other media to make the media bootable.

Search the Microsoft TechNet Library at *technet.microsoft.com/en-us/library/default.aspx* for information about each tool. Write a short paragraph about each tool that you think would be helpful to someone learning about the tool or how to use it. Share this information with others in your class. As you share with others, everyone gets a better understanding of these tools used to automate a Windows deployment.

>> REAL PROBLEMS, REAL SOLUTIONS

REAL PROBLEM 1-1: A Corrupted Windows Installation

As a PC support technician for a small organization, it's your job to support the PCs, the small network, and the users. One of your coworkers, Jason, comes to you in a panic. His Windows 7 system won't boot, and he has lots of important data files in several locations on the drive. He has no idea in which folder some of the files are located. Besides the applications data he's currently working on, he's especially concerned about losing e-mail addresses, e-mail, and his Internet Explorer Favorites links.

After trying everything you know about recovering Windows 7, you conclude the OS is corrupted beyond repair. Based on what you have learned in this chapter, list the steps you would take to reinstall Windows 7 and recover all the data that Jason needs.

Securing and Troubleshooting Windows 7

When a new Windows operating system comes on the market, PC support technicians must quickly learn to install, maintain, secure, and troubleshoot it. This chapter helps you do just that. The good news is that there are not a lot of new things to learn in Windows 7 if you already know how to support Windows Vista. Some view Windows 7 as Windows Vista made leaner and faster. It really is fundamentally the same operating system with a few changes. In this chapter, you will see for yourself the many tools, utilities, and methods that are the same, and learn about the exceptions where changes have been made from Windows Vista to Windows 7.

In the chapter, you'll first look at the many tools used to support Windows 7 and Vista and compare their similarities and differences. Then you'll look at the best practices used to secure a Windows 7 computer. Finally, you'll learn about the changes Windows 7 makes in the tools you use when there is a problem starting Windows 7.

Notes Appendix B contains several labs to accompany this chapter. Take the time to work through these labs to get some real-time experience using Windows 7 to secure and troubleshoot the OS.

WINDOWS 7 UTILITIES AND TOOLS TO SUPPORT THE OS

A+
220-701
2.2, 2.5,
3.2, 3.3,
3.4

Windows 7 utilities and tools used to support the OS are similar or the same as those used in Windows Vista. Table 2-1 is a summary of the Windows 7 tools and how they differ from the Vista tools.

Windows 7 Tool	Description	Similar Vista Tool
Action Center	◢ Accessed from the taskbar and Control Panel ◢ Central location for several security and maintenance tools	The Security Center in Vista is less powerful than the Action Center
Advanced Boot Options menu	◢ Accessed by pressing the F8 key when Windows first starts to load ◢ Use several options on this menu to help you troubleshoot boot problems	Same as Windows 7, but with one fewer option
Backup and Restore	◢ Accessed from the Start menu ◢ Use it to back up and restore data folders and the system image, which is a backup of the entire Windows volume ◢ You have control over which folders to back up ◢ Can only make one backup schedule	In Vista, you have little control over which folders to back up. The backup of the entire Windows volume is called the Complete PC Backup.
Boot logging	◢ Press F8 at startup and select from the Advanced Boot Options menu ◢ Use events logged to the Ntbtlog.txt file to investigate the source of an unknown startup error	Same as Windows 7
Bootcfg (Bootcfg.exe)	◢ Enter Bootcfg at a command prompt ◢ Use it to view the contents of the Boot.ini file	Same as Windows 7
Chkdsk (Chkdsk.exe)	◢ At a command prompt, enter Chkdsk with parameters ◢ Use it to check and repair errors on a volume or logical drive. If critical system files are affected by these errors, repairing the drive might solve a startup problem.	Same as Windows 7
Command prompt window	◢ Accessed from Start menu ◢ Allows you to enter commands at a command prompt ◢ An elevated command prompt window is available with administrator privileges	Same as Windows 7
Compatibility Mode	◢ Accessed from the Action Center or the program file's shortcut menu ◢ Use it to resolve issues that prevent legacy applications or drivers from working	Vista calls the tool the Program Compatibility Wizard. It is accessed from the program file's shortcut menu.
Computer Management (Compmgmt.msc)	◢ Accessed from Control Panel or you can enter Compmgmt.msc at a command prompt ◢ Use it to access several snap-ins to manage and troubleshoot a system	Same as Windows 7

Table 2-1 Windows 7 utilities and tools compared to Vista utilities and tools

Windows 7 Tool	Description	Similar Vista Tool
Control Panel	◢ Accessed from the Start menu ◢ Use it to change many settings that affect Windows, applications, hardware, and users. These settings include system, security, network, Internet, hardware, installed programs, user accounts, display, desktop, clock, language, and ease-of-access settings.	In Vista, Control Panel functions the same as in Windows 7 although it is organized slightly differently
Defrag.exe	◢ At a command prompt, enter Defrag with parameters ◢ Use it to defragment a drive to improve drive performance and access time	Same as Windows 7
Device Driver Roll Back	◢ Accessed from Device Manager ◢ Use it to replace a driver with the one that worked before the current driver was installed	Same as Windows 7
Device Manager (Devmgmt.msc)	◢ Accessed from the System window or System Properties window ◢ Use it to verify that a driver is installed with no errors, to solve problems with hardware devices, to update device drivers, to view driver signing, and to disable and uninstall a device	Same as Windows 7
Disk Cleanup (Cleanmgr.exe)	◢ Accessed from a drive's properties window or by entering Cleanmgr at a command prompt ◢ Use it to delete unused files to make more disk space available; not enough free hard drive space can slow down a system and cause boot problems	Same as Windows 7
Disk Defragmenter (Dfrg.msc)	◢ Accessed from a drive's properties window ◢ Use it to defragment a volume to improve performance ◢ By default, defragmentation is automatically set to happen weekly	Same as Windows 7
Disk Management (Diskmgmt.msc)	◢ Accessed from the Computer Management console, or enter Diskmgmt.msc at a command prompt ◢ Use it to view and change partitions on hard drives and to format drives	Same as Windows 7
Driver Verifier (verifier.exe)	◢ Enter verifier.exe at a command prompt ◢ Use it to identify a driver that is causing a problem. The tool puts stress on selected drivers, which causes the driver with a problem to crash. ◢ The tool can be used to solve system lock-up errors and blue screen errors caused by a corrupted driver for an input or output device	Same as Windows 7

Table 2-1 Windows 7 utilities and tools compared to Vista utilities and tools (continued)

2

A+ 220-701

A+
220-701
2.2, 2.5,
3.2, 3.3,
3.4

Windows 7 Tool	Description	Similar Vista Tool
Error Reporting	◢ Accessed from Control Panel or Action Center ◢ This automated Windows service displays error messages when an application or hardware error occurs ◢ A history of past problems and solutions is maintained	**Vista calls the tool Problem Reports and Solutions**
Event Viewer (Eventvwr.msc)	◢ Accessed from the Computer Management console ◢ Check the Event Viewer logs for error messages to help you investigate all kinds of hardware, security, and system problems ◢ When a system locks up or freezes and you must restart it, check Event Viewer to see if it has reported a hardware failure	Same as Windows 7
File Signature Verification Tool (Sigverif.exe)	◢ At a command prompt, enter Sigverif with parameters ◢ Searches for installed drivers that are unsigned and stores results of the search in \Windows\ sigverif.txt ◢ When a device driver or other software is giving problems, use it to verify that the software has been approved by Microsoft	Same as Windows 7
Group Policy (Gpedit.msc)	◢ At a command prompt, enter Gpedit.msc to open the Local Group Policy Editor ◢ Use it to display and change policies controlling users and the computer ◢ Not available with Home editions of Windows 7	Same as Windows 7
Last Known Good Configuration	◢ Press F8 at startup and select from the Advanced Boot Options menu ◢ Use this tool when Windows won't start normally and you want to revert the system to an earlier state before a change was made in a Windows setting, driver, or application that is causing problems	Same as Windows 7
Memory Diagnostics (mdsched.exe)	◢ Enter mdsched.exe in a command prompt window or access it from Windows RE ◢ Use it to test memory	Same as Windows 7
Microsoft Management Console (mmc.exe)	◢ Accessed by using the program filename ◢ Use it to create customized consoles from individual tools called snap-ins	Same as Windows 7

Table 2-1 Windows 7 utilities and tools compared to Vista utilities and tools (continued)

Windows 7 Tool	Description	Similar Vista Tool
Network and Sharing Center	⊿ Accessed from the taskbar or the Control Panel ⊿ Centralized location to manage wired and wireless network connections and network security settings	In Vista, the Network and Sharing Center window is organized differently and does not include the link to the Internet Options box
Performance Monitor (perfmon.exe)	⊿ Can be accessed from the Action Center, or, at a command prompt, enter perfmon.exe or perfmon.msc ⊿ Use it to view information about performance to help you identify a performance bottleneck	Vista combines the Resource Monitor and the Performance Monitor in one window and calls it the Reliability and Performance Monitor
Programs and Features window	⊿ Accessed from Control Panel ⊿ Use it to uninstall, repair, or update software or certain device drivers that are causing a problem	Same as Windows 7
Registry Editor (Regedit.exe)	⊿ At a command prompt, enter Regedit ⊿ Use it to view and edit the registry	Same as Windows 7
Resource Monitor (resmon.exe)	⊿ Can be accessed from the Action Center, or, at a command prompt, enter resmon.exe ⊿ Use it to view information about how hardware (CPU, memory, hard drive, and network) are used by processes and services. It can help you identify a process or service that is hogging resources.	Vista combines the Resource Monitor and the Performance Monitor in one monitoring tool and calls it the Reliability and Performance Monitor
Safe Mode	⊿ At startup, press F8 and select the option from the Advanced Boot Options menu ⊿ Use it when Windows does not start or starts with errors. Safe Mode loads the Windows desktop with a minimum configuration. In this minimized environment, you can solve a problem with a device driver, display setting, or corrupted or malicious applications.	Same as Windows 7
Services console (Services.msc)	⊿ At a command prompt, enter Services.msc ⊿ Use the console to stop or start a service that runs in the background	Same as Windows 7
System Configuration Utility (Msconfig.exe)	⊿ At a command prompt, enter Msconfig ⊿ Troubleshoot the startup process by temporarily disabling startup programs and services	Same as Windows 7
System File Checker (Sfc.exe)	⊿ At a command prompt, enter Sfc with parameters ⊿ Use it to verify the version of all system files when Windows loads; useful when you suspect system files are corrupted, but you can still access the Windows desktop	Same as Windows 7

Table 2-1 Windows 7 utilities and tools compared to Vista utilities and tools (continued)

A+
220-701
2.2, 2.5,
3.2, 3.3,
3.4

Windows 7 Tool	Description	Similar Vista Tool
System image	◢ The system image is created using the Backup and Restore tool and is a backup of the entire Windows volume. Incremental backups of the system image can be maintained. ◢ Use Windows RE to reinstall the OS from the system image. Windows RE can be launched from the repair disc, the Windows setup DVD, or the Advanced Boot Options menu ◢ When restoring the system using the system image, all data on the Windows volume is lost	Vista uses the Complete PC Backup instead of the system image
System Information (Msinfo32.exe)	◢ At a command prompt, enter Msinfo32 ◢ Use it to display information about hardware, applications, and Windows	Same as Windows 7
System Information (Systeminfo.exe)	◢ At a command prompt, enter Systeminfo ◢ A text-only version of the System Information window. To direct that information to a file, use the command Systeminfo.exe > Myfile.txt. Later the file can be printed and used to document information about the system.	Same as Windows 7
System repair disc	◢ The repair disc is created using the Backup and Restore tool ◢ Use the disc to boot the Windows Recovery Environment (Windows RE). You can then launch the process to restore the Windows volume using a system image.	Vista does not offer the option to create a repair disc
System Restore	◢ Accessed from the Start menu, when loading Safe Mode, or in Windows RE ◢ Use it to restore the system to a previously working condition. It restores the registry, some system files, and some application files from a previously saved restore point. ◢ Restore points are managed using the System Protection tab on the System Properties box	Same as Windows 7
Task Killing Utility (Tskill.exe)	◢ At a command prompt, enter Tskill with parameters ◢ Use it to stop or kill a process or program currently running. Useful when managing background services such as an e-mail server or Web server.	Same as Windows 7

Table 2-1 Windows 7 utilities and tools compared to Vista utilities and tools (continued)

Windows 7 Tool	Description	Similar Vista Tool
Task Lister (Tasklist.exe)	▲ At a command prompt, enter Tasklist ▲ Use it to list currently running processes similar to the list provided by Task Manager	Same as Windows 7
Task Manager (Taskman.exe)	▲ Right-click the taskbar and select Start Task Manager ▲ Use it to list and stop currently running processes. Useful when you need to stop a locked-up application.	Same as Windows 7
Task Scheduler	▲ Accessed from Control Panel ▲ Schedules a program to run at the times you specify	Same as Windows 7
User Account Control (UAC) box	▲ Configure settings through the Control Panel or Action Center ▲ Use it to prevent malware from installing and protect Windows settings ▲ An administrator has control over when the UAC box is used	In Vista, an administrator has less control over when the box is used and the box is used more often in Vista. Settings are configured through Control Panel.
Windows Defender	▲ Accessed from Control Panel ▲ Monitors activity and alerts you if a running program appears to be malicious or damaging the system	Same as Windows 7 except the Vista version includes Software Explorer
Windows Firewall	▲ Accessed from Control Panel or the Network and Sharing Center ▲ Service runs in the background to prevent or filter uninvited communication from another computer	The Vista Windows Firewall windows are organized differently from Windows 7, but functionality is the same
Windows Recovery Environment (recenv.exe)	▲ Windows RE is a lean OS launched from the hard drive, the system repair disc, or the Windows 7 setup DVD ▲ Windows RE provides a graphic and command-line interface ▲ Use the tool to solve Windows startup problems	Windows RE is launched in Vista from the Vista setup DVD. The tools in Windows RE work the same in Vista as in Windows 7.
Windows Update (Wupdmgr.exe)	▲ Accessed from the Start menu ▲ Use it to update Windows by downloading the latest patches from the Microsoft Web site	Same as Windows 7
Windows XP Mode	▲ Installed in a virtual machine (VM) and then accessed from the Start menu ▲ Use it to run legacy applications that do not work in Compatibility Mode	Not available in Windows Vista

Table 2-1 Windows 7 utilities and tools compared to Vista utilities and tools (continued)

Notes Windows Vista Software Explorer is not included in Windows 7. Use the System Configuration Utility (Msconfig) instead when you want to control the processes that launch at startup.

2

A+ 220-701

A+ 220-702 2.1

Looking at Table 2-1, you can see many similarities between the tools in Windows 7 and those in Vista. This fact should build your confidence that if you can support Vista, learning to support Windows 7 will be easy. Now let's look at command-line tools, directory structures, and file systems and see how, they, too, are similar in Windows 7 and Vista.

📝 **Notes** To learn how you can use the Windows 7 Performance Monitor to help identify a system performance bottleneck, see Lab 2.1 in Appendix B.

COMMAND-LINE TOOLS

Windows 7 uses the same command prompt utilities as does Vista. Several of these commands and their uses are listed below:

- *Telnet* – A Windows command-line client/server application that allows an administrator or other user to control a computer remotely.
- *Ping* – A command used to troubleshoot network connections by verifying that the host can communicate with another host on the network.
- *Ipconfig* – Displays the IP address of the host and other configuration information. The command can also be used to release and renew the IP address.
- *Dxdiag* – Displays information about hardware and diagnoses problems with DirectX.
- *Cmd* – Launches a command prompt window.
- *Xcopy* – Used to copy files and folders and has many options to control how the copy operation will proceed.
- *Net* – Several commands that all begin with Net, such as Net use and Net config. These commands are used to display information about network connections, make connections, and solve network connectivity problems.
- *Tracert* – Traces the route from the host to a destination host and displays each hop to the destination.
- *Netstat* – Displays statistics about network activity. It can be used to identify a program hogging network resources.
- *Nslookup* – Reads and displays information from the Internet name space used to resolve domain names and their corresponding IP addresses kept by a DNS server.

A+ 220-702 2.2

DIRECTORY STRUCTURES IN WINDOWS 7

You also need to know that startup folders are the same as they are in Windows Vista. These folders are:

- **For individual users:** C:\Users*username*\AppData\Roaming\Microsoft\Windows\ Start Menu\Programs\Startup
- **For all users:** C:\ProgramData\Microsoft\Windows\Start Menu\Programs\Startup

❓ **To Learn More** The directory structure of Windows 7 folders and files for user files, system files, program files, fonts, temporary files, and offline files and folders is the same as for Vista. To see a complete list of these locations, see pages 642 to 644 in Chapter 13 of *A+ Guide to Managing and Maintaining Your PC*, 7th edition, or pages 174 to 176 in Chapter 4 of *A+ Guide to Software*, 5th edition.

A+
220-702
2.3

STORAGE DEVICES AND FILE SYSTEMS IN WINDOWS 7

One way Windows 7 has improved performance over XP and Vista is that it is engineered to make fewer reads and writes to the hard drive. Windows 7 is also designed to perform better when using solid state drives (SSDs). If you want to get even better performance with Windows 7, consider installing Windows 7 on an SSD rather than a regular hard drive. An SSD performs in the range of 11 MB/sec to 130 MB/sec. A traditional magnetic hard drive performs in the range of 0.8 MB/sec to 2 MB/sec. Performance for an SSD is about the same when reading and writing sectors randomly or when reading and writing contiguous sectors. Because of this fact, Windows 7 disables defragmentation for these SSDs.

For USB flash drives, consider using the exFAT file system. The exFAT file system, also called the FAT64 file system, is structured the same as the older FAT32 file system. It uses a 64-bit wide, one-column file allocation table (FAT) that tracks each cluster on the volume. exFAT does not use as much overhead as the NTFS file system and is designed to handle very large files, such as those used for multimedia storage. It is compatible with flash media devices such as smart cards and USB flash drives, and is designed to work with other operating systems and devices. For example, you can use a smart card formatted with exFAT in a Mac or Linux computer or in a digital camcorder, camera, or smart phone.

When you format an internal drive using Disk Management, the partitioning and formatting wizard offers the option to use the exFAT or the NTFS file system. Use NTFS for very large hard drives or drives that will contain the Windows installation. When Disk Management formats a removable storage device, it offers the option to use exFAT, FAT16, FAT32, or NTFS. Use exFAT for USB flash drives and other removable flash media.

SECURING WINDOWS 7 RESOURCES

A+
220-702
4.2

As a PC support technician, you are likely to be responsible for securing the resources on a Windows 7 computer in a small office, home office, or small business. These small networks are most likely set up as a peer-to-peer network rather than a domain. Security on a domain is controlled by a domain controller such as Windows Server 2008 and managed by a network administrator. In small peer-to-peer networks, security for each PC is maintained at the local level by Windows installed on each PC. Following is a quick overview of how security at the local level is managed by Windows 7, which uses many of the same methods as does Windows Vista.

To control access to resources on the local computer:

▲ *User accounts.* User accounts on the local computer can require passwords and sometimes other methods to authenticate the user when the user logs onto the system.
▲ *Permissions.* Permissions are assigned to data folders and programs stored on the computer to authorize which logged-on local users have access to these resources.

To control access to resources on the network:

▲ *Homegroup security.* A Windows homegroup has one password that is used for each computer in the homegroup. Folders and files are then shared with the homegroup and are available to any user of any homegroup computer. Homegroup security is considered weak security because homegroup files and folders are available to all users in the homegroup. A homegroup is easy to set up and is appropriate when all users in a small network can be trusted with access to all shared resources in the homegroup. Windows Vista does not support a homegroup, and a homegroup is only available when the Windows 7 network location is set to a Home network.

2

A+ 220-702

> **Notes** To learn more about the security provided by homegroups, see Lab 2.2 in Appendix B.

◢ *Workgroup security with user accounts and passwords.* User accounts and passwords provide a more secure method of controlling access to network resources than does a homegroup. Using the workgroup method, you can control which user has access to which folders or files shared on the network, and this is the method used by Windows Vista. Use this method when you have both Windows 7 and Vista computers on a network or you are using all Windows 7 computers and want more control over who has access to specific resources than that provided by a homegroup.

◢ *Shared permissions.* Shared permissions are assigned to folders and files stored on the computer to authorize which users on the network have access to these resources.

> **Notes** To learn how to set permissions and shared permissions in Windows 7, see Lab 2.3 in Appendix B.

◢ *User Account Control (UAC) box.* Use the UAC box to help prevent malware from installing itself and to protect the Windows configuration and other settings. The UAC box in Windows 7 is not as annoying as it is in Vista and only appears when you are making a significant change to the system. You learned how to manage the UAC box in Chapter 1.

◢ *Windows Firewall.* Windows Firewall controls communication initiated from a remote computer on the local network or the Internet.

◢ *Antivirus and antispyware software.* Antivirus and antispyware software is installed and runs in the background to protect the system from malicious attacks. Windows 7 provides two products for this purpose: Windows Security Essentials and Windows Defender.

◢ *Hardware firewall.* Most small networks are protected by a hardware firewall that stands between the Internet and the local network to guard against uninvited communication. Many small routers serve double duty as a hardware firewall, wireless access point, and gateway to the Internet.

◢ *Advanced encryption technologies.* An organization might implement advanced encryption technologies to protect sensitive data. Windows 7 Professional, Ultimate, and Enterprise editions support the Encrypting File System (EFS) to encrypt data folders. Windows 7 Ultimate and Enterprise editions support BitLocker Encryption to encrypt an entire internal hard drive. In addition, Windows 7 BitLocker To Go can be used to encrypt data on external hard drives or USB flash drives. These encryption technologies can be especially important for laptop computers that employees use when traveling. If the laptop is stolen, the data can still be protected from thieves.

> **? To Learn More** To learn more about encrypting technologies in Windows, see pages 1053 through 1060 in Chapter 20 in *A+ Guide to Managing and Maintaining Your PC*, 7th edition, and pages 559 through 566 in Chapter 11 in *A+ Guide to Software*, 5th edition.

◢ *Scheduled backups.* Scheduled backups protect data from corruption or accidental deletions. If the original data is lost, it can be recovered from backups. You learned how to set up a scheduled backup in Chapter 1.

A+
220-702
4.2

▲ *User training.* User training is often the most overlooked security measure. Users need to practice locking down their workstations when they step away, not writing down or giving out passwords, not removing sensitive data from the workplace, carefully watching their laptops when they travel, and making sure antivirus software is running and updated on their home computers used for telecommuting.

> **Notes** To lock down a computer, press the **Windows key** and **L**. Another method is to press **Ctrl-Alt-Del** and select **Lock this computer** from the menu that appears. A third method is to click **Start**, click the right arrow next to **Shutdown**, and then click **Lock**. Regardless of the method used, the computer is locked, and a user password is required to unlock the computer.

In reviewing all these security measures, know that the Windows 7 tools to implement these measures work the same as they do in Vista with a few minor exceptions. Two of these exceptions that you need to be aware of are how to set up a homegroup and how the Windows Firewall windows are organized.

SETTING UP A HOMEGROUP

Recall that you can approach sharing resources on a small peer-to-peer network (one that is not part of a domain) using one of two methods: a Windows 7 homegroup or a workgroup with user accounts and passwords. And it is possible to use both methods on the same network.

When you have Windows 7, Vista, and XP computers sharing resources on a network, you must use a workgroup rather than a homegroup because Vista and XP do not support homegroups. To set up a workgroup, use the System Properties window to assign the same workgroup name to each computer that will be sharing resources. Then share individual files and folders with all users or specific users on the network. The procedures to share files and folders are the same as those of Vista and will not be repeated here.

> **? To Learn More** To learn more about sharing files and folders without applying strict security measures, see pages 1009 through 1013 in Chapter 19 in *A+ Guide to Managing and Maintaining Your PC*, 7th edition, and pages 515 through 519 in Chapter 10 in *A+ Guide to Software*, 5th edition.
>   To learn more about sharing files and folders using strict security measures and controls, see pages 1040 through 1048 in Chapter 20 in *A+ Guide to Managing and Maintaining Your PC*, 7th edition, and pages 546 through 554 in Chapter 11 in *A+ Guide to Software*, 5th edition.

A homegroup is an easy way to share resources on a network of Windows 7 computers when strict security measures are not required. Follow these steps to learn how to set up a homegroup:

1. To open the Network and Sharing Center window, click the network icon in the taskbar. In the network status box, click **Open Network and Sharing Center**. The Network and Sharing Center opens (see Figure 2-1).

2. Under the area *View your active networks*, you can view the network location which will be a Home network, Work network, or Public network. If it does not read Home network, click **Work network** or **Public network** to change the location.

3. The Set Network Location box appears (see Figure 2-2). Click **Home network**.

2

A+ 220-702

A+
220-702
4.2

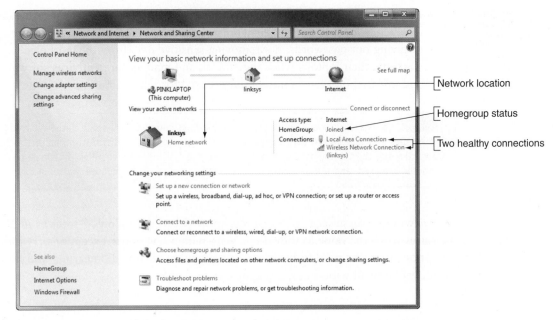

Figure 2-1 Network and Sharing Center
Courtesy: Course Technology/Cengage Learning

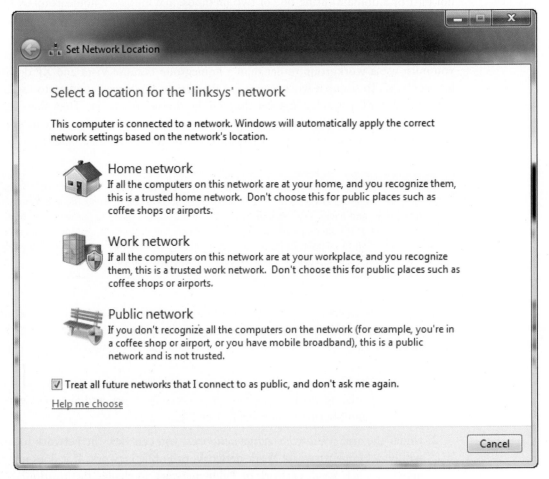

Figure 2-2 Set the network location
Courtesy: Course Technology/Cengage Learning

Windows determines if a homegroup exists on the network and if the computer has already joined it. Depending on the situation, three things can happen:

▲ *A homegroup exists and the computer has not yet joined the homegroup.* In this situation, the HomeGroup window looks like the one in Figure 2-3. Do the following to join the homegroup:

1. In Figure 2-3, click **Join now**. The Join a Homegroup window in Figure 2-4 appears. Select the Windows libraries to share with the homegroup and decide if local printers will be shared. Click **Next**.

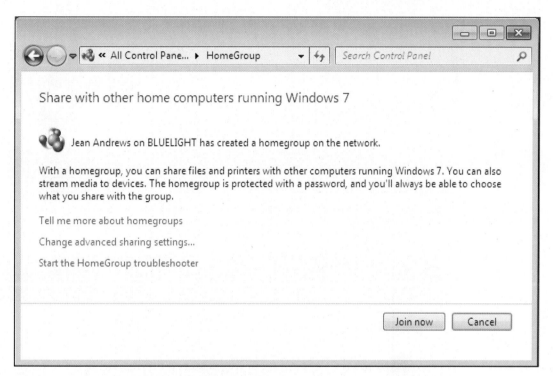

Figure 2-3 The computer does not belong to a homegroup
Courtesy: Course Technology/Cengage Learning

2. On the next screen, enter the homegroup password and click **Next**. Then click **Finish** and close the HomeGroup window.

> **Notes** If you don't know the homegroup password, go to another computer on the network that belongs to the homegroup and open the HomeGroup window. Click **View or print the homegroup password**.

▲ *A homegroup has not yet been set up on the network.* In this situation, the Set Network Location box appears (see Figure 2-5). To set up a new homegroup, do the following:

1. Click **View or change HomeGroup settings**.

2. The Create a HomeGroup window shown in Figure 2-6 appears. Select what you want to share and click **Next**.

A+
220-702
4.2

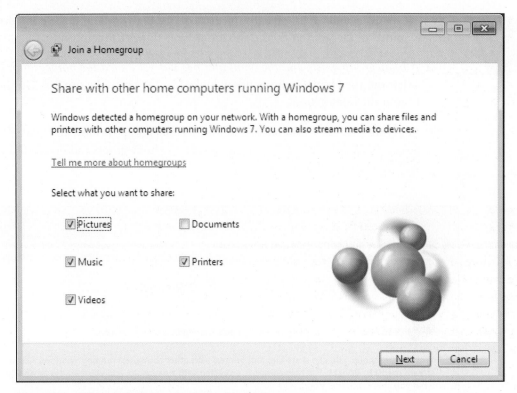

Figure 2-4 Select the resources to share with the homegroup
Courtesy: Course Technology/Cengage Learning

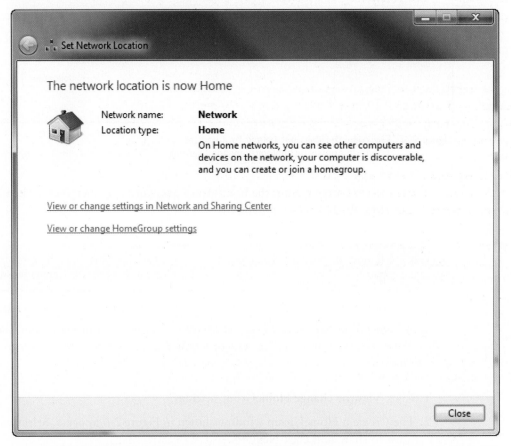

Figure 2-5 The network location is changed to a Home network
Courtesy: Course Technology/Cengage Learning

A+
220-702
4.2

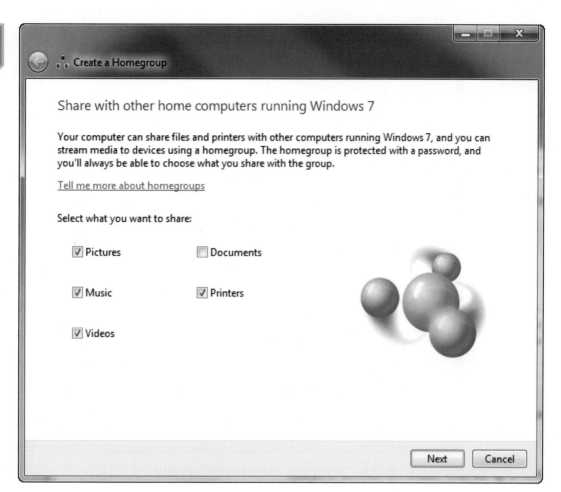

Figure 2-6 Create a homegroup
Courtesy: Course Technology/Cengage Learning

3. On the next screen (see Figure 2-7), write down the suggested password or enter your own and click **Finish**. The homegroup is created.

▲ *The computer has already joined a homegroup.* In this situation, the HomeGroup window appears as shown in Figure 2-8. In this window, you can change the libraries and printers that belong to the homegroup, leave the homegroup, or change the password to the homegroup.

> **Notes** To view and change homegroup settings after a computer has joined a homegroup, click **HomeGroup** in the left pane of the Network and Sharing Center window.

Follow these steps to verify that you can access resources on the network that are shared to the homegroup and change the resources that are shared:

1. Open **Windows Explorer**. Listed under Homegroup are all computers connected to the network that belong to the homegroup. Click one computer to see its shared resources (see Figure 2-9). You can then drill down to homegroup folders and files shared by this computer.

2. Notice in Figure 2-9 that resources on the BLUELIGHT computer shared with the homegroup include additional folders other than Windows default libraries and printers. Any folder or file can be shared with the homegroup. For example, to share

A+
220-702
4.2

Figure 2-7 Windows recommends a password to the homegroup
Courtesy: Course Technology/Cengage Learning

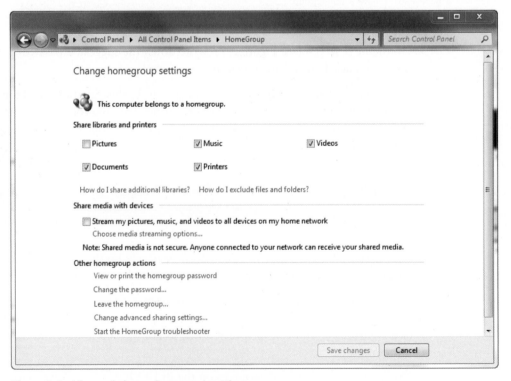

Figure 2-8 View and change homegroup settings
Courtesy: Course Technology/Cengage Learning

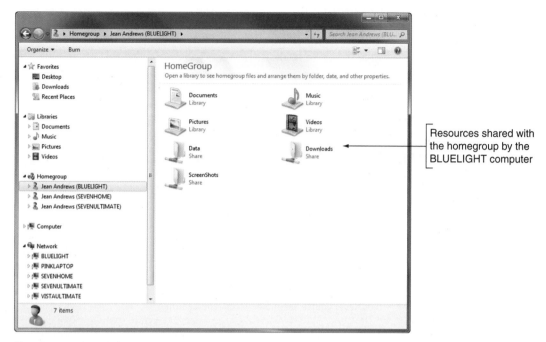

Resources shared with the homegroup by the BLUELIGHT computer

Figure 2-9 Use Windows Explorer to see resources shared to the homegroup by other computers on the network
Courtesy: Course Technology/Cengage Learning

the folder C:\Data with the homegroup, right-click the folder and point to **Share with** from the shortcut menu. To give read and write access to users on the network, click **Homegroup (Read/Write)** from the menu (see Figure 2-10).

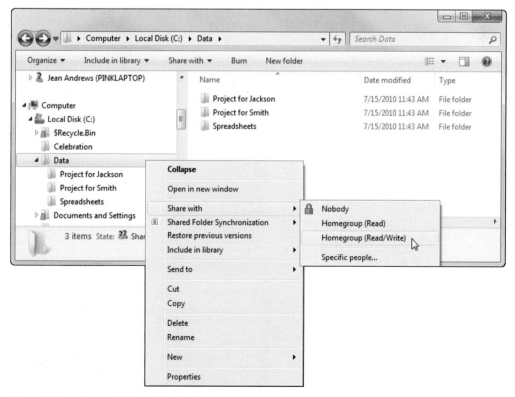

Figure 2-10 Share a folder with the homegroup
Courtesy: Course Technology/Cengage Learning

A+
220-702
4.2

3. When you select the shared folder in Windows Explorer, the two-person share icon appears in the status bar at the bottom of Windows Explorer (see Figure 2-11).

Figure 2-11 A folder shared with the homegroup shows the two-person shared icon in the status bar of Windows Explorer
Courtesy: Course Technology/Cengage Learning

In summary, use a homegroup when you don't need to control which users have access to specific folders shared on the network. If you need more precise security, use a workgroup with user accounts and passwords used for share permissions.

You can also use a combination of homegroup and workgroup security on the same network. For example, a user on the network who does not have a user account on the BLUELIGHT computer shown in Figure 2-12 attempts to drill down to the \Financial folder shown in the figure and discovers that access is denied. This user cannot access this folder

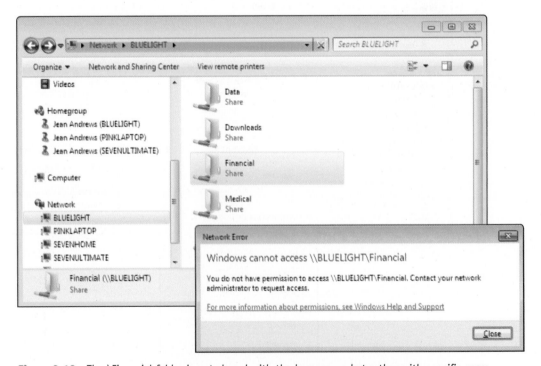

Figure 2-12 The \Financial folder is not shared with the homegroup but rather with specific users
Courtesy: Course Technology/Cengage Learning

A+
220-702
4.2

because the folder has been assigned share permissions for specific users and she is not one of these users. She can, however, drill down to the \Data or \Downloads folder contents because these folders are shared with the homegroup rather than specific users.

CONFIGURING WINDOWS FIREWALL

Windows Firewall in Windows 7 functions about the same way as it does in Vista. However, the windows in Windows Firewall are organized differently. Follow these steps to find out how to configure Windows Firewall in Windows 7:

1. Click the network icon in the taskbar. In the network status box, click **Open Network and Sharing Center**. The Network and Sharing Center opens (refer back to Figure 2-1).

2. In the lower part of the left pane, click **Windows Firewall**. The Windows Firewall window opens (see Figure 2-13).

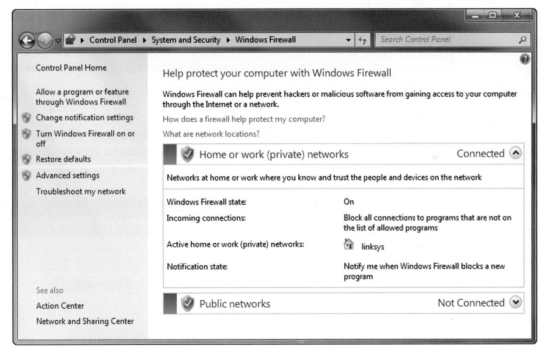

Figure 2-13 Windows Firewall shows the computer currently connected to a private network
Courtesy: Course Technology/Cengage Learning

3. To change firewall settings, click **Turn Windows Firewall on or off** in the left pane. The Windows Firewall Customize Settings window appears (see Figure 2-14).

4. Using this window, you can turn Windows Firewall on or off and control how incoming connections (those not initiated by this computer) are handled. To provide more security on a public network, check **Block all incoming connections, including those in the list of allowed programs**. After you have made your changes, click **OK**. The icon beside Public networks in the Windows Firewall window changes from a green check mark to a red circle with a line through it indicating increased security.

2

A+ 220-702

A+
220-702
4.2

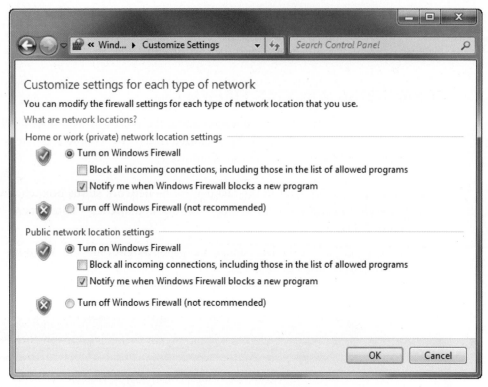

Figure 2-14 Customize settings for a private or public network
Courtesy: Course Technology/Cengage Learning

5. To change the programs allowed through the firewall, in the Windows Firewall window shown in Figure 2-13, click **Allow a program or feature through Windows Firewall**. The Allowed Programs window appears (see Figure 2-15).

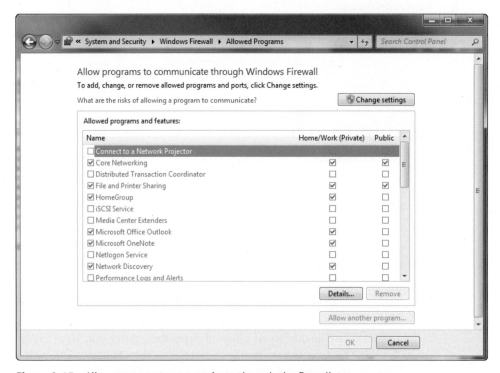

Figure 2-15 Allow programs to communicate through the firewall
Courtesy: Course Technology/Cengage Learning

6. Find the program you want to allow to initiate a connection from a remote computer to this computer. In the right side of the window, click either *Home/Work (Private)* or *Public* to indicate which type of network the program is allowed to use. If you don't see your program in the list, click **Allow another program** to see more programs or to add your own. When you are finished making changes, click **OK** to return to the Windows Firewall window.

SOLVING WINDOWS 7 STARTUP PROBLEMS

Windows 7 uses the same startup files and processes as does Windows Vista. In addition, Windows 7 and Vista use the same two main tools for solving problems with startup processes: the Advanced Boot Options menu and the Windows Recovery Environment (Windows RE).

> **? To Learn More** To learn more about the startup files and steps to start Windows and the tools used to solve startup problems, see pages 765 through 783 in Chapter 15 in *A+ Guide to Managing and Maintaining Your PC*, 7th edition, and pages 299 through 317 in Chapter 6 in *A+ Guide to Software*, 5th edition.

The most significant difference between Windows 7 tools and Vista tools for troubleshooting Windows startup problems is that the Windows Recovery Environment (Windows RE) is installed on the hard drive by default in Windows 7 and is, therefore, available to you from the Advanced Boot Options menu. A less significant change is that Windows 7 gives you the opportunity to create a Windows 7 repair disc from which you can load Windows RE. Both changes are discussed in this part of the chapter.

LAUNCH WINDOWS RE FROM THE ADVANCED BOOT OPTIONS MENU

Windows RE is a lean operating system that can be launched to solve Windows startup problems after other tools available on the Advanced Boot Options menu have failed to solve the problem. In Windows 7, Windows RE is installed on the hard drive and available on the Advanced Boot Options menu.

> **Notes** In Windows Vista, Windows RE is not installed on the hard drive by default, but you can manually install it so that it is accessible from the Advanced Boot Options menu.

If Windows 7 fails to start and the hard drive is still intact, follow these steps to use the Advanced Boot Options window which includes Windows RE:

1. Press **F8** while the computer boots. The Advanced Boot Options menu appears (see Figure 2-16). Notice this menu is the same as that of Windows Vista except for the first option.

2. Deciding which tool on the Advanced Boot Options menu to use first depends on the nature of the problem you are solving. Use the same strategies for these tools as you have used with Vista, including the Last Known Good Configuration to solve problems with Windows settings and software installations and Safe Mode to solve problems with malware and corrupted drivers. If these solutions don't solve your problem, the next option to use is Windows RE.

3. To launch Windows RE, select the first option, **Repair Your Computer**. A System Recovery Options box appears (see Figure 2-17). Select your keyboard input method and click **Next**.

A+
220-702
2.4

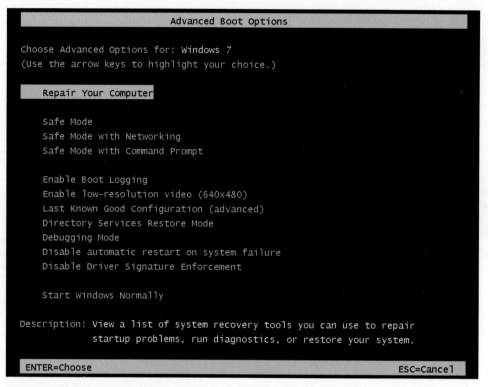

```
                    Advanced Boot Options

Choose Advanced Options for: Windows 7
(Use the arrow keys to highlight your choice.)


    Repair Your Computer

        Safe Mode
        Safe Mode with Networking
        Safe Mode with Command Prompt

        Enable Boot Logging
        Enable low-resolution video (640x480)
        Last Known Good Configuration (advanced)
        Directory Services Restore Mode
        Debugging Mode
        Disable automatic restart on system failure
        Disable Driver Signature Enforcement


        Start Windows Normally

Description: View a list of system recovery tools you can use to repair
            startup problems, run diagnostics, or restore your system.


ENTER=Choose                                          ESC=Cancel
```

Figure 2-16   Press F8 during the boot to launch the Windows 7 Advanced Boot Options menu
Courtesy: Course Technology/Cengage Learning

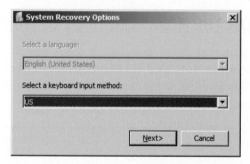

Figure 2-17   Select your language and keyboard preferences
Courtesy: Course Technology/Cengage Learning

4. In the next box (see Figure 2-18), select your user account that has administrative privileges, enter your password, and click **OK**.

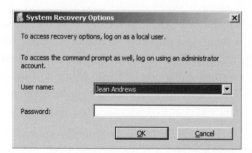

Figure 2-18   Select an account with administrative privileges
Courtesy: Course Technology/Cengage Learning

5. The System Recovery Options window appears where you can select a recovery tool (see Figure 2-19). The tools in this window are the same as those in Vista.

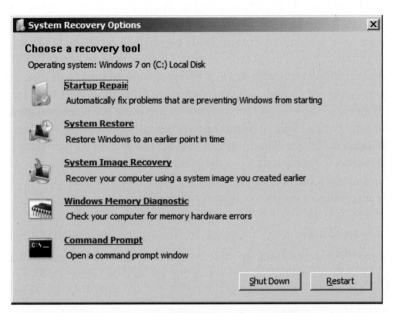

Figure 2-19 Recovery tools in Windows RE
Courtesy: Course Technology/Cengage Learning

When deciding which tool to use in Figure 2-19, always use the least intrusive tool first. In other words, fix the problem while making as few changes to the system as possible. Use the Windows RE tools in this order:

1. Try Startup Repair. This option is the least intrusive. It does not change user data or installed applications and can sometimes fix a startup problem.

2. If you suspect memory might be a problem, use the Windows Memory Diagnostic to identify a corrupted memory module.

3. Use System Restore to restore the system to a previously saved restore point. This option can sometimes fix a problem with a corrupted device driver, corrupted Windows settings, or corrupted programs. The process will not affect user data.

4. If you suspect the hard drive is corrupted, use the Command Prompt option to open a command prompt window and then use Chkdsk to check the hard drive for errors. You can also use commands in the Command Prompt window to restore a corrupted registry from a backup.

> **? To Learn More** To learn more about commands to repair a corrupted registry and other commands useful to solve startup problems, see pages 781 through 783 in Chapter 15 in *A+ Guide to Managing and Maintaining Your PC,* 7th edition, and pages 315 through 317 in Chapter 6 in *A+ Guide to Software,* 5th edition.

5. Use the System Image Recovery as a last resort. It uses a previously created system image to restore the entire Windows volume to this image. Be aware that everything on the Windows volume will be erased and replaced with the system image. Before you use this option, make every attempt to recover from the hard drive any data files that have not yet been backed up.

**A+
220-702
2.4**

CREATE AND USE THE WINDOWS 7 REPAIR DISC

The Windows 7 system repair disc is used to launch Windows RE. You can create the disc during some installations of Windows 7, and at any time after the installation. The disc is useful if Windows 7 will not start, you cannot launch Windows RE from the hard drive, and you do not have a Windows 7 setup DVD handy for launching Windows RE.

A 32-bit Windows 7 installation will create a 32-bit version of the repair disc, and a 64-bit Windows 7 installation will create a 64-bit version of the repair disc. A repair disc created on one computer can be used on a different computer even if they are using different editions of Windows 7 as long as both computers are using the same version of Windows 7 (32-bit or 64-bit). For example, if you create the disc on a computer running a 64-bit version of Windows 7 Home Premium, you can use the disc on a computer running a 64-bit version of Windows 7 Professional. On the other hand, you cannot use this same disc on a computer running a 32-bit version of Windows 7 Home Premium.

Follow these directions to create the system repair disc:

1. Open Control Panel.

2. In Control Panel, click **Back up your computer** in the System and Security group. The Backup and Restore window opens (see the left side of Figure 2-20).

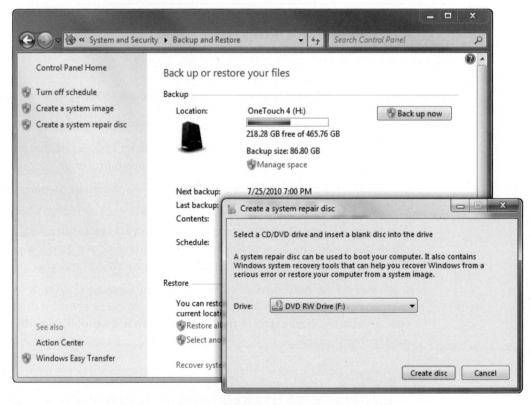

Figure 2-20 Use the Backup and Restore window to create a system repair disc
Courtesy: Course Technology/Cengage Learning

3. In the left pane, click **Create a system repair disc**. The Create a system repair disc box appears (see the right side of Figure 2-20).

4. Insert a blank CD or DVD in the optical drive. Select the optical drive you are using and click **Create disc**. The disc is created.

A+
220-702
2.4

5. Windows displays a message reminding you to label the disc (see Figure 2-21). Be sure to include on the label if the disc is to be used for a 32-bit or 64-bit version of Windows 7.

Figure 2-21 Label the Windows 7 repair disc as a 32-bit or 64-bit disc
Courtesy: Course Technology/Cengage Learning

To use the disc to repair a failed Windows installation, boot from the disc. When you follow the directions on-screen, the Windows Recovery Environment loads (refer back to Figure 2-19). Use the Windows RE tools to repair the system.

Notes To learn more about the repair disc and Windows RE, see Labs 2.4 and 2.5 in Appendix B.

>> CHAPTER SUMMARY

▲ Commands and tools that work the same way in Windows 7 and Vista include the Advanced Boot Options menu, Boot logging, Bootcfg, Chkdsk, the Command Prompt, Computer Management, Defrag, Device Driver Roll Back, Device Manager, Disk Cleanup, Disk Defragmenter, Disk Management, File Signature Verification Tool, Driver Verifier, Event Viewer, Group Policy, Last Known Good Configuration, Memory Diagnostics, Microsoft Management Console, Programs and Features window, Registry Editor, Safe Mode, the Services console, System Configuration Utility, System File Checker, System Information, System Restore, Task Killing Utility, Task Lister, Task Manager, Task Scheduler, and Windows Update.

▲ Use the exFAT file system for USB flash drives and other removable media. Use the NTFS file system for large hard drives.

▲ The Windows 7 Action Center is more powerful than the Vista Security Center and replaces it.

▲ Windows 7 Backup and Restore gives you more control over which folders to back up than does the Vista Backup and Restore utility.

▲ A system image in Windows 7 is called a Complete PC Backup in Vista.

◢ The Performance Monitor and Resource Monitor in Windows 7 are two different tools, but in Vista they are combined in the Vista Reliability and Performance Monitor.

◢ An administrator has more control over when the UAC box appears in Windows 7 than she does in Vista.

◢ Vista Software Explorer is not included in Windows 7. Use the System Configuration Utility instead.

◢ Windows Firewall in Windows 7 is organized differently than in Vista, but has the same functionality.

◢ Windows Security Essentials is antivirus software available for Windows 7 and Windows Defender is antispyware embedded in Windows 7.

◢ The Advanced Boot Options menu looks and works the same way in Windows 7 as Vista except one new option is included. This option is Repair Your Computer, and it can be used to launch the Windows Recovery Environment (Windows RE).

◢ Three ways to start Windows RE in Windows 7 are by using the Windows 7 repair disc, from the Advanced Boot Options menu, and by booting from the Windows 7 setup DVD.

◢ The Windows 7 repair disc used to launch Windows RE can be created using the Backup and Restore utility. The disc is created to work for either a 32-bit or 64-bit OS depending on the OS used to create it.

◢ A repair disc can be used for any edition of Windows 7 so long as the version (32-bit or 64-bit) is the same.

>> KEY TERMS

exFAT – A file system similar to the older FAT32 file system and uses a 64-bit wide, one-column file allocation table (FAT) that tracks each cluster on the volume. exFAT is compatible with the Mac and Linux operating systems and is well suited for handling large multimedia files on removable drives. *Also called* the FAT64 file system.

system repair disc – A disc created by the Windows 7 Backup and Restore Tool that can be used to boot the system and launch Windows RE. You can use the disc to restore the Windows volume using a previously created system image.

>> REVIEWING THE BASICS

1. What key do you press during startup to launch the Advanced Boot Options menu?

2. A backup of the entire Windows 7 volume is called the _____.

3. What is the program filename and extension of the Windows 7 Performance Monitor?

4. Which file system is the best choice when formatting a USB flash drive that you plan to use on both a Mac and PC?

5. What is the difference between folder permissions and folder shared permissions?

6. Which Windows tool blocks communication that was initiated by another computer?

7. What is the program filename and extension of the System Configuration utility?

8. What tool in Windows Vista, used to temporarily disable a startup program, is not available in Windows 7?

9. What tool in Windows 7 can be used to temporarily disable a startup program?

10. What software in Windows 7 is used to block spyware?

11. What two tools are used in Windows 7 for encrypting sensitive data on internal hard drives?

12. What option on the Windows 7 Advanced Boot Options menu is not found by default on the Vista Advanced Boot Options menu?

13. Which option on the Windows RE options menu should be used only as a last resort? Why?

14. Can a Windows 7 repair disc created on a 32-bit installation of Windows 7 Ultimate be used to solve a startup problem on a 64-bit installation of Windows 7 Home Premium? Why or why not?

15. Which utility can you use in Windows 7 to create the Windows 7 repair disc?

>> THINKING CRITICALLY

1. When you step away from your computer for a few minutes, how do you lock it down so another user cannot steal your data?

   a. Perform a system shutdown by clicking Start and then Shut down.

   b. Put the system in hibernation by clicking Start and Hibernate.

   c. Disconnect the monitor cable from the computer.

   d. Lock the computer by clicking the Win key and the L key at the same time.

2. Windows refuses to start and gives a blue screen error about a failed device driver. The system worked yesterday and no new drivers have been installed. What is the first thing you should try?

   a. Boot from the Windows setup DVD and select Startup Repair from the Windows RE menu.

   b. Press F8 at startup and select Last Known Good Configuration from the Advanced Boot Options menu.

   c. Create a Windows 7 repair disc on another computer and use it to launch Windows RE on this computer.

   d. Press F8 at startup and select Safe Mode from the Advanced Boot Options menu.

3. When a driver is giving problems in Windows, which tool offers the least intrusive solution?

   a. Device Manager

   b. System Restore

   c. System Image Recovery

   d. Last Known Good Configuration

>> *HANDS-ON PROJECTS*

<u>**PROJECT 2-1:**</u> Researching Running Processes

Boot to the Windows desktop and then use Task Manager to get a list of all the running processes on your machine. Use the Windows 7 Snipping Tool to save and print the Task Manager screens showing the list of processes. Next, boot the system into Safe Mode and use Task Manager to list running processes. Which processes that were loaded normally are not loaded when the system is running in Safe Mode?

<u>**PROJECT 2-2:**</u> Practicing Launching Programs at Startup

Do the following to practice launching programs at startup, listing the steps you took for each activity:

1. Configure Scheduled Tasks to launch Notepad each time the computer starts and any user logs on. List the steps you took.

2. Put a shortcut in a startup folder so that any user launches a command prompt window at startup.

3. Restart the system and verify that both programs are launched. Did you receive any error messages?

4. Remove the two programs from the startup process.

<u>**PROJECT 2-3:**</u> Editing and Restoring the Registry

Practice editing and restoring the registry by changing the name of the Recycle Bin on the Windows desktop. When editing the registry, always back up a key before you edit it so that you can backtrack if you make a mistake. You can back up a key by exporting the key to the Windows desktop. Later, if you need to restore this key from backup, you can import the exported key. Follow these steps to back up the registry key and then edit a subkey in this key that contains the name of the Recycle Bin:

1. Using the Registry Editor, export the registry key HKEY_CURRENT_USER\Software\Microsoft\Windows\ CurrentVersion\Explorer to an export file stored on the desktop.

2. To change the name of the Recycle Bin on the Windows 7 desktop for the currently logged-on user, click the following subkey, which holds the name of the Recycle Bin: HKEY_CURRENT_USER\Software\Microsoft\Windows\CurrentVersion\Explorer\CLSI D\645FF040-5081-101B-9F08-00AA002F954E.

3. The data entry for this key is set to "value not set," which means the default name, Recycle Bin, is used. To enter a new name for the Recycle Bin, in the right pane, double-click **Default**. The Edit String box appears. The Value data text box in the dialog box should be empty. If a value is present, you selected the wrong value. Check your work and try again.

4. Enter a new name for the Recycle Bin, for example "Trash Can." Click **OK**.

5. Move the Registry Editor window so that you can see the Recycle Bin on the desktop. Don't close the window.

6. Right-click the desktop and select **Refresh** on the shortcut menu. The name of the Recycle Bin changes.

7. To restore the name to its default value, in the Registry Editor window, again double-click **Default**, delete your entry, and click **OK**.

8. To verify the change is made, refresh the Windows desktop. The Recycle Bin name should return to its default value.

9. Exit the Registry Editor and then delete the exported registry key stored on the desktop.

10. From these directions, you can see that changes made to the registry take effect immediately. Therefore, take extra care when editing the registry. If you make a mistake and don't know how to correct a problem you create, then you can restore the key that you exported by exiting the Registry Editor and double-clicking the exported key.

2

PROJECT 2-4: Using the Microsoft Management Console

Using the Microsoft Management Console in a Windows 7 system, follow the step-by-step directions on pages 694 through 696 in Chapter 14 of the *A+ Guide to Managing and Maintaining Your PC,* 7th edition, or pages 228 through 230 in Chapter 5 in *A+ Guide to Software,* 5th edition, to create a customized console. Put two snap-ins in the console: Device Manager and Event Viewer. Store a shortcut to your console on the Windows 7 desktop. Do the steps to create a console in Windows Vista differ from those of Windows 7?

PROJECT 2-5: Finding Windows Utilities

The following table lists some important Windows utilities covered in this chapter. Fill in the right side of the table with the filename and path of each utility. (*Hint*: You can use Windows Explorer or Search to locate files.)

Utility	Filename and Path in Windows 7	Filename and Path in Windows Vista
Task Manager		
System Configuration Utility		
Services Console		
Computer Management		
Microsoft Management Console		
Event Viewer		
Performance Monitor		
Registry Editor		

>> *REAL PROBLEMS, REAL SOLUTIONS*

REAL PROBLEM 2-1: Cleaning Up Startup and Speeding Up a Sluggish System

Using a Windows 7 computer that has a sluggish startup or runs slowly, solve the problem by cleaning up the startup process. Take detailed notes of each step you take and the results. (If you are having a problem finding a computer with a sluggish startup, consider offering your help to a friend, a family member, or a nonprofit organization.) To clean up startup, follow the eleven step-by-step directions and explanations under the heading *Improving Windows Performance* on pages 710 through 730 in Chapter 14 of the *A+ Guide to Managing and Maintaining Your PC,* 7th edition, or pages 244 through 264 in Chapter 5 in *A+ Guide to Software,* 5th edition. These eleven steps are written for Windows Vista and will need some slight adjusting for Windows 7 as follows:

1. Perform routine maintenance.

2. Check if the hardware can support the OS.

3. Check for performance warnings.

4. Check the Reliability Monitor. (In Windows 7, this tool is called the Resource Monitor.)

5. Disable the indexer for Windows Search.

6. Disable the Aero interface.

7. Disable the Vista sidebar. (Windows 7 does not have the sidebar. In Windows 7, remove any gadgets from the desktop.)

8. Plug up any memory leaks.

9. Consider disabling the UAC box.

10. Consider using ReadyBoost.

11. Clean Windows startup.

Labs for Chapter 1: Installing and Maintaining Windows 7

Labs included in this appendix:

- **Lab 1.1:** Determine Hardware Compatibility with Windows 7
- **Lab 1.2:** Install or Upgrade to Windows 7
- **Lab 1.3:** Navigate and Customize Windows 7
- **Lab 1.4:** Manage Windows 7 Libraries
- **Lab 1.5:** Download and Use Microsoft Security Essentials
- **Lab 1.6:** Install and Use Windows XP Mode and Windows Virtual PC

LAB 1.1 DETERMINE HARDWARE COMPATIBILITY WITH WINDOWS 7

OBJECTIVES

The goal of this lab is to help you determine if your hardware is compatible with Windows 7. After completing this lab, you will be able to:

◢ Use the Windows 7 Upgrade Advisor to find out if your system qualifies for Windows 7

◢ Use Device Manager to identify system components

◢ Use the Windows 7 Compatibility Center to investigate compatibility problems

MATERIALS REQUIRED

This lab will require the following:

◢ Windows Vista or XP operating system

◢ Internet access

LAB PREPARATION

Before the lab begins, the instructor or lab assistant needs to do the following:

◢ Verify that Windows starts with no errors

◢ Verify that Internet access is available

ACTIVITY BACKGROUND

If your PC is currently running Windows Vista, it can probably run Windows 7. If your PC is currently running Windows XP, it might be able to run Windows 7. In either case, to verify that Windows 7 supports your hardware, you can run the Windows 7 Upgrade Advisor or you can search for your hardware online using the Windows 7 Compatibility Center Web site. Both methods are covered in this lab. You will first use the Windows 7 Upgrade Advisor. Then you will use Windows Vista or XP Device Manager to inventory installed hardware devices and search for these in the Windows 7 Compatibility Center.

The Compatibility Center Web site lists devices and applications that have been approved for Windows 7 by Microsoft and offers suggestions for solving incompatibility problems. Keep in mind that not all product manufacturers submit their drivers or applications for testing by Microsoft. If you don't find a hardware device listed on the site, check the hardware manufacturer's Web site for a Windows 7 driver that you can download from the site. If the Web site claims the device works under Windows 7, most likely it will.

> **ESTIMATED COMPLETION TIME: 45 Minutes**

 Activity

To download, install, and run the Windows 7 Upgrade Advisor, follow these steps:

> **Notes** Web sites change from time to time, so you might need to adjust the following steps to accommodate Microsoft changes to its site.

1. Log onto the Windows Vista or XP system using a user account with administrative privileges.

2. Plug in and turn on any USB devices such as a USB printer or external hard drive that you want the Upgrade Advisor to check.

3. To open Internet Explorer, click **Start** and click **Internet Explorer**. The Internet Explorer window opens.

4. To navigate to the Microsoft Web site, enter the following URL and press **Enter**: **windows.microsoft.com/en-us/windows/downloads/upgrade-advisor**

5. Scroll down near the bottom of the page and click **Download the Windows 7 Upgrade Advisor**.

6. On the next page, click **Download**.

7. The File Download – Security Warning box appears. Click **Run**. The file is saved to a temporary folder.

8. If necessary, respond to the UAC box by clicking **Continue**.

9. The Windows 7 Upgrade Advisor window opens. To agree to the license terms, select **I accept the license terms** and click **Install**. The installation process begins.

10. A window appears informing you that the installation is complete. Click **Close** to close this window.

11. To launch the Upgrade Advisor, click **Start**, click **All Programs**, and click **Windows 7 Upgrade Advisor**. If necessary, respond to the UAC box.

12. The Windows 7 Upgrade Advisor launches. On the opening window, click **Start check**.

13. A report appears in the Windows 7 Upgrade Advisor window (see Figure A-1). Verify that no problems are found. List any problems that might prevent your system qualifying for Windows 7:

_____

_____

_____

A

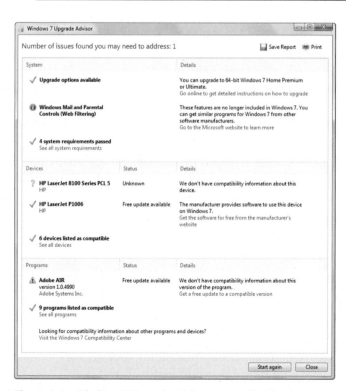

Figure A-1   Windows 7 Upgrade Advisor reports that hardware and applications qualify for Windows 7 with one issue to address
Courtesy: Course Technology/Cengage Learning

14. To verify the system requirements, click **See all system requirements**. The system requirements display. Answer these questions:

   ◢ What upgrade options are available for your system?

   _____

   ◢ Does your graphics adapter support the Aero user interface?

   _____

   ◢ What is the speed of your CPU? Does it qualify for Windows 7?

   _____

   _____

   ◢ How much RAM does your system have?

   _____

   ◢ How much free space is available on drive C:? Is there enough free space on drive C: to install Windows 7?

   _____

   _____

15. Close the Windows 7 Upgrade Advisor.

16. Close your browser.

Another tool you can use to find out if your computer qualifies for Windows 7 is the Windows 7 Compatibility Center. First, you need to use Device Manager to inventory your hardware devices. Follow these steps:

1. To open Device Manager, click **Start**, right-click **Computer**, and select **Properties**. On the System window, click **Device Manager**. (In Windows XP, right-click **My Computer** and select **Properties**. On the System Properties window, click the **Hardware** tab, and then click **Device Manager**.) If necessary, respond to the UAC box. The Device Manager window opens.

2. In Device Manager, devices are arranged by category. To see what kind of video adapter is installed on your system, click the **+** (plus sign) to the left of **Display adapters**.

3. Right-click your video adapter and select **Properties** from the shortcut menu. Record the information displayed about the model and manufacturer:

   _____

   _____

   _____

4. Click **Cancel** to close the Properties box.

5. Use Device Manager to find similar information for your network adapter, wireless adapter, or sound card, and record that information here:

   _____

6. Close the Device Manager window.

7. Printers are not listed in the Device Manager, but it's important to verify these devices qualify for Windows 7. Open the Vista **Printers** window or the XP **Printers and Faxes** window. Right-click the icon for each installed printer and select **Properties** from the shortcut menu. In the Properties window, locate the brand and model of the printer. You might find this information on the General tab or the About tab. Record the information about each installed printer here:

8. Close the **Properties** window. Close the Vista **Printers** window or the XP **Printers and Faxes** window.

9. USB devices other than USB printers must also qualify for Windows 7. List all USB devices installed on your system. List the type device, the manufacturer, and model number of the device:

Now that you have a list of devices installed on your system, check the Windows 7 Compatibility Center to see if Windows 7 supports these devices.

1. Open your browser and go to this URL:

    www.microsoft.com/windows/compatibility/windows-7/en-us/default.aspx

2. The opening page at this site is shown in Figure A-2. Notice you can search for either Software or Hardware. You can begin a search by entering the product name in the search box or by drilling down into a specific category on the screen. Click the **Hardware** tab to search for hardware.

3. It is important that your network adapter qualify for Windows 7, so let's begin there. Mouse over the Networking icon and select **Ethernet Adapters** from the shortcut menu.

4. Select the brand of your network adapter from the list in the left pane. Then scroll through the list until you find your adapter. Does your network adapter qualify for Windows 7?

5. To try a new way to search, enter the brand and model of your video adapter in the search box near the top of the page and click **Search**. If Microsoft cannot locate the exact model, a list from which you can choose appears. Confirm that you have found the right adapter. Does your video adapter qualify for Windows 7?

A

Figure A-2   Use the Windows 7 Compatibility Center to verify that your hardware and software qualify for
Windows 7
Courtesy: Course Technology/Cengage Learning

6. Check all devices in your list. If you don't find a device listed, use a search engine such
   as *www.google.com* and find the product manufacturer's Web site. Search the Web site
   for information about the product being compatible with Windows 7. List below any
   devices that do not qualify for Windows 7:

   _____

   _____

   _____

7. Close the browser window.

Do the following to determine if your system meets the minimum or recommended hardware requirements for Windows 7.

1. Windows 7 requires a minimum of 1 GB of RAM for a 32-bit installation and 2 GB of
   RAM for a 64-bit installation. To find out how much RAM your system has, click **Start**,
   right-click **Computer** (for XP, **My Computer**), and select **Properties**. The amount of
   installed RAM is displayed. Write the amount here:

   _____

2. Windows 7 requires a processor rated at least 1 GHz, although faster is recommended.
   The System window (or System Properties window for XP) displays the processor
   rating. Record that rating here:

   _____

3. Close the Vista System window or the XP System Properties window.

4. Windows 7 requires at least 16 GB of free hard drive space for a 32-bit installation and 20 GB of free space for a 64-bit installation. To find out how much free space is on your drive, use Disk Management. Click **Start**, right-click **Computer** (for XP, **My Computer**), and select **Manage** from the shortcut menu. If necessary, respond to the UAC box. Then click **Disk Management**. The Disk Management window similar to Figure A-3 appears.

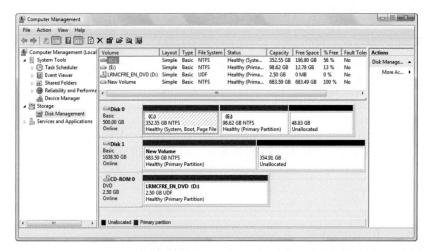

Figure A-3   Use the Disk Management window to find out information about installed hard drives and free space on the drives
Courtesy: Course Technology/Cengage Learning

5. Adjust the column widths and window width so that you can see the column labeled Free Space, as shown in Figure A-3. Answer these question:

   ◢ How much free space is on drive C?

   _____

   ◢ How much free space is on other partitions?

   _____

6. Close the Computer Management window.

REVIEW QUESTIONS

1. Do your system and all its installed devices qualify for Windows 7? If not, list any components or devices that do not qualify:

   _____

   _____

   _____

   _____

   _____

   _____

A

2. If your system does not have an internal DVD or CD drive and is not connected to a network, can you still install Windows 7 from a DVD? What device can you use for the installation?

_____

3. Why is it possible for a device to not be listed on the Windows 7 Compatibility Center, but the device still work under Windows 7?

_____

4. Is it possible to install a USB device in a Windows 7 computer when you can only obtain Windows 98 drivers for the device?

_____

5. If you cannot find Windows 7 drivers for your network card but the other components in a system qualify for Windows 7, how can you still install Windows 7?

_____

_____

LAB 1.2 INSTALL OR UPGRADE TO WINDOWS 7

OBJECTIVES

The goal of this lab is to help you install or upgrade to Windows 7. After completing this lab, you will be able to:

◢ Plan an upgrade or installation

◢ Identify the benefits of an upgrade or clean installation

◢ Install or upgrade to Windows 7

MATERIALS REQUIRED

This lab will require the following:

◢ Windows Vista operating system

◢ Access to drivers or Internet access for downloading drivers

◢ Windows 7 setup DVD or installation files at another location. Any edition of Windows 7 will work in this lab so long as the edition of Vista installed on the PC qualifies for the edition of Windows 7 you are using. See Chapter 1 for a table of acceptable upgrade paths to Windows 7.

◢ Product key from Windows 7 package

◢ A storage medium for updated device drivers

LAB PREPARATION

Before the lab begins, the instructor or lab assistant needs to do the following:

◢ Verify that Windows starts with no errors

◢ Provide each student with access to the Windows 7 installation files and product key

◢ Verify that any necessary Windows 7 drivers are available

ACTIVITY BACKGROUND

Performing an upgrade to Windows 7 takes less time than performing a clean installation of Windows 7. It also has the advantage that user preferences and settings are not lost and applications are left in working condition. However, if the Windows Vista system is giving trouble, performing a clean installation is a good idea so that current problems don't follow you into the new installation.

You can perform an upgrade installation of Windows 7 when certain editions of Windows Vista are installed. You cannot upgrade from Windows XP to Windows 7. For this lab, you upgrade from Windows Vista using a Vista Home, Business, or Ultimate edition that qualifies for the upgrade edition of Windows 7 you are installing. Installing or upgrading an operating system isn't difficult. Careful planning can minimize or eliminate many of the headaches some users have experienced when upgrading to a new operating system.

ESTIMATED COMPLETION TIME: 90 Minutes

 Activity

Before installing Windows 7, do your research and download device drivers that are compatible with Windows 7. You might need to go to the manufacturer's Web site for each device, such as scanners, printers, network adapters, memory card readers, cameras, and so on, to see if they are compatible with Windows 7. If the manufacturer provides a Windows 7 driver, you need to download the files to a storage media. Also, when planning an upgrade, recording information in a table, such as Table A-1, is helpful. Follow these steps to create a plan and prepare for a Windows 7 upgrade on your computer:

1. Using information given in Lab 1-1, compile information in the first row of Table A-1.

Things to Do	Further Information
Does the PC meet the minimum or recommended hardware requirements?	**CPU:** **RAM:** **Free space on the hard drive:**
Have you checked all your applications to verify that they qualify for Windows 7 or need patches to qualify?	**Applications that need to be upgraded:**
Have you checked the Microsoft Web site to verify that all your hardware qualifies?	**Hardware that needs to be upgraded:**
Have you decided how you will join a network?	**Computer name:** **Workgroup name:** **Domain name:**
Do you have the product key available?	**Product key:**
Have you backed up critical data?	**Location of backup files:**
Is your hard drive ready?	**Size of the hard drive partition:**
Did you run Chkdsk and Defrag?	**Free space on the partition:**

Table A-1 Things to do and information to collect when planning a Windows upgrade

2. Compare your information to the Windows 7 requirements in Table A-2.

◢ Does your system meet the minimum requirements?

Component or Device	For 32-bit Windows 7	For 64-bit Windows 7
Processor	1 GHz or faster, 32-bit (x86) or 64-bit (x64)	1 GHz or faster, 64-bit (x64)
Memory (RAM)	1 GB	2 GB
Free hard drive space	16 GB	20 GB
Video device and driver	DirectX 9 device with WDDM 1.0 or higher driver	DirectX 9 device with WDDM 1.0 or higher driver

Table A-2   Windows 7 minimum hardware requirements

3. Make a list of important applications on your system and verify that they are compatible with Windows 7:

_____

_____

_____

_____

_____

4. Install any application upgrades or patches that are available from the manufacturers' Web sites.

Verify that your devices qualify for Windows 7. Do the following:

1. It is important for you to be able to access the Internet during and after the Windows 7 installation. Verify that you have Windows 7 drivers for your network or wireless adapter. If you don't have the drivers, download Windows 7 drivers for the adapter from the manufacturer's Web site. List the location of any drivers you downloaded:

_____

_____

_____

2. Gather network-specific information in preparation for the installation. Answer the following:

   ◢ How is your IP address configured?

   _____

   ◢ For a static IP address, what is the IP address?

   _____

   ◢ What is the workgroup name or domain name of the network?

   _____

◢ What is your computer name?

_____

◢ Record the workgroup or domain name and the computer name in Table A-1.

3. Make sure you have the product key needed for the installation and record it in Table A-1.

4. Back up all critical data files, that is, any work you or others have stored on your computer that you can't afford to lose. Don't forget to back up Internet Explorer favorites, e-mail data, and your e-mail address book. Record backup locations in Table A-1.

You're now ready to begin the installation. The following steps are representative of a typical upgrade. Don't be alarmed if your experience differs slightly. Use your knowledge to solve any problems on your own, and ask your instructor for help if you get stuck. You might want to record any differences between these steps and your own experience. Also, record any decisions you make and any information you enter during the installation process.

1. Use your antivirus software to scan the system for viruses. After the scan is finished, make sure you disable any automatic scans and close the antivirus program.

2. Close any open applications such as Instant Messenger or Internet Explorer.

3. Insert the Windows 7 DVD. The AutoPlay dialog box appears. Click **Run setup.exe**. The Setup program starts. Click **Install now**.

4. On the next screen, if you are connected to the Internet, click **Go online to get the latest updates for installation (recommended)**. If you use this option, you'll need to stay connected to the Internet throughout the installation.

5. On the next window, accept the license agreement and click **Next**.

6. On the next screen, select the type of installation you want, either an upgrade or a clean install. Select **Upgrade**.

7. Windows 7 setup searches for compatibility issues that might prevent the OS from installing or might disable a Vista feature that is currently installed. If compatibility issues are found, setup displays a Compatibility Report window showing a message about the issue. List any error messages or warning messages that display for your installation and indicate if the message is an error message (causing the installation to terminate) or is only a warning message (allowing the installation to continue):

_____

_____

_____

8. When you receive an error message that causes the installation to terminate, you must resolve the problem and begin the installation again. If you received an error message, describe how you resolved the problem:

_____

_____

_____

9. If you received a warning message, click **Next** in the Compatibility Report window to continue with the installation.

A

10. If no error messages appeared or you received a warning message, the installation continues. Wait while files are copied and the PC reboots several times. At the end of this process, a screen appears asking for the product key. Enter the product key and click **Next**.

11. The next screen asks how you want to handle Windows updates. Click **Use recommended settings**.

12. On the next screen, verify the time and date settings are correct and click **Next**.

13. On the next screen, select the network setting, either Home network, Work network, or Public network. Select the one appropriate for your situation.

14. If you select a Home network and you know the password for the homegroup, on the next screen, enter it and click **Next**. If you don't know the homegroup password, click **Skip**.

15. Finally, a logon screen appears. Log in with your user ID and password. The Windows 7 desktop loads and the installation is complete.

REVIEW QUESTIONS

1. Was the Windows 7 installation a success? If so, what did you find to be most challenging about the upgrade process?

_____

2. Using Disk Management, find out how much free space is on drive C:. Also, how much space did the Windows 7 installation use?

_____

_____

3. What is the size of the Windows.old folder? What is the purpose of this folder?

_____

_____

4. When performing a clean install of Windows, setup gives you the opportunity to create a user account and password during the installation process. Why do you think setup skipped this step in an upgrade installation?

_____

LAB 1.3 NAVIGATE AND CUSTOMIZE WINDOWS 7

OBJECTIVES

The goal of this lab is to help you become familiar with navigating and customizing the Windows 7 user interface. After completing this lab, you will be able to:

◢ Manage windows using the Aero Peek, Snap, and Shake features of Windows 7

◢ Manage and customize the Windows 7 taskbar and desktop

MATERIALS REQUIRED

This lab will require the following:

◢ Windows 7 operating system, any edition

LAB PREPARATION

Before the lab begins, the instructor or lab assistant needs to do the following:

◢ Verify that Windows starts with no errors

ACTIVITY BACKGROUND

Becoming proficient at navigating a new operating system can require some time and effort. Although many similarities exist between Windows 7 and Windows Vista, some changes in the user interface have been made. In this lab, you'll explore these changes. You'll also learn how to customize the notification area of the Windows 7 taskbar.

ESTIMATED COMPLETION TIME: 30 Minutes

 Activity

Do the following to explore how Windows 7 manages open windows and the taskbar:

1. Open **Internet Explorer** and navigate to your favorite music site.

2. In Internet Explorer, click the **New Tab** button to open a new tab (see Figure A-4). Navigate to your favorite news site.

Figure A-4 Click the New Tab button to open a new tab in Internet Explorer
Courtesy: Course Technology/Cengage Learning

3. To open the Calculator, click **Start, All Programs, Accessories,** and **Calculator.**

4. To open the Solitaire game, click **Start, All Programs, Games,** and **Solitaire.**

5. You now have three applications open. Move your mouse pointer over each application icon in the taskbar. Notice the thumbnail is a live presentation: If you make a change in the application window while the thumbnail is displayed, the change appears in the thumbnail.

6. To see a Jump List, right-click the Internet Explorer icon in the taskbar. The Jump List appears showing Web sites you have visited frequently. Click one of these sites in the Jump List. Notice that a new tab opens in Internet Explorer and you now have three tabs open.

7. Mouse over the Internet Explorer icon in the taskbar. Live thumbnails of all three tabs display. Click one of these thumbnails. This tab now becomes the active tab in Internet Explorer.

8. Right-click the **Solitaire** icon in the taskbar. The Jump List appears.

9. On the Jump List, select **Pin this program to taskbar.**

10. Close the **Solitaire** window. Because you have pinned the Solitaire program to the taskbar, its icon remains in the taskbar even after the program is closed.

11. Click the **Solitaire** icon in the taskbar to open the Solitaire game again.

12. To unpin the Solitaire game from the taskbar, right-click the **Solitaire** icon in the taskbar and select **Unpin this program from taskbar** from the Jump List.

A

Follow these steps to see how Aero Peek, Snap, and Shake work:

1. Mouse over the rectangle at the far right of the taskbar. Notice how all windows disappear and you have a full view or peek of the desktop.

2. Click in this rectangle to minimize all windows.

3. Click again in the rectangle to restore the windows.

4. Move the cursor into the title bar of the **Solitaire** window. Press and drag until the window touches the top of the screen and then release the mouse button. The Aero Snap feature causes the window to maximize.

5. Move the cursor over the title bar of the **Solitaire** window, press and drag the window down an inch or so, and release the mouse button. The window size is restored.

6. Using the Internet Explorer window, move the cursor over the title bar, press and drag the window so that your cursor is on the far-left side of the window and release the mouse button. The window snaps to the left side of the screen.

7. Using the same action, snap the window to the right side of the screen.

8. Position your cursor over the **Internet Explorer** title bar, and then press and hold the mouse button while you shake the window. All windows are minimized except this one (the feature is called Aero Shake). Shake the window again to restore other windows.

Flip view and 3D flip work the same in Windows 7 as they do in Vista. Follow these steps to see these views:

1. To see how the flip view works, press **Alt+Tab**. Hold down the **Alt** key to keep the flip view open. Use your **Tab** key to move from one application to the next. When you release the Alt key, the last application you tabbed to is in front.

2. To learn about the 3D flip view, press **Win+Tab**. Hold down the **Win** key and use the **Tab** key to move through all open applications. When you release the Win key, the last selected application is in front.

Do the following to learn how to use the notification area:

1. To view the system clock and calendar, click the date and time displayed in the notification area. Click the arrows to the left and right of the month to scroll through the calendar. Click outside the clock area to close the clock and calendar window.

2. To see hidden icons in the notification area, click the up arrow to the immediate left of the notification area. In the box that appears over the arrow (see Figure A-5), click an icon to open it.

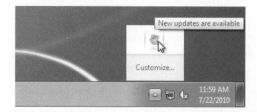

Figure A-5   The up arrow in the notification area shows hidden icons
Courtesy: Course Technology/Cengage Learning

3. To customize the notification area, click the up arrow to the immediate left of the notification area and then click **Customize** in the box that appears. The Notification Area Icons window appears (see Figure A-6).

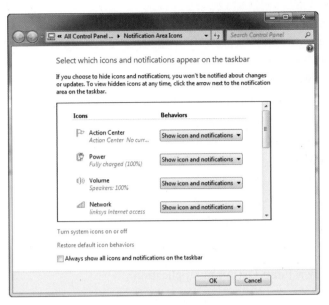

Figure A-6   Manage the notification area icons
Courtesy: Course Technology/Cengage Learning

4. The window shows a list of icons that can be controlled. List the icons shown in your window:

_____

_____

_____

_____

_____

_____

_____

_____

_____

5. The Behaviors of each icon are available in a drop-down menu to the right of the icon. List the three Behaviors available for each icon:

_____

_____

_____

6. Click **Cancel** to close the Notification Area Icons window.

A

Follow these steps to see how you can add a gadget to the Windows 7 desktop:

1. Right-click anywhere on the Windows desktop and select **Gadgets** from the shortcut menu. The Gadgets window appears.

2. Press and drag the **Weather** gadget to the Windows desktop.

3. Drag the gadget to different places on the desktop. Vista gadgets stayed in the Vista sidebar, but Windows 7 gadgets can go anywhere on the desktop.

4. Right-click the **Weather** gadget and select **Close gadget** from the shortcut menu.

5. Close all open windows.

REVIEW QUESTIONS

1. How do you open a new tab in Internet Explorer?

   _____

2. How do you display a Jump List for an application?

   _____

3. How do you pin an application's icon to the taskbar?

   _____

   _____

   _____

4. How do you quickly minimize all open windows except one?

   _____

   _____

5. How can you quickly cause a window to take up the right half of the screen?

   _____

   _____

   _____

LAB 1.4 MANAGE WINDOWS 7 LIBRARIES

OBJECTIVES

The goal of this lab is to help you learn to use Windows 7 libraries to help manage user folders. After completing this lab, you will be able to:

◢ Understand the structure of the Documents library

◢ Create a library and add three folders to it

MATERIALS REQUIRED

This lab will require the following:

◢ Windows 7 operating system, any edition

LAB PREPARATION

Before the lab begins, the instructor or lab assistant needs to do the following:

◢ Verify that Windows starts with no errors

ACTIVITY BACKGROUND

A Windows 7 library is a collection of one or more folders and their contents. These folders can be located in any storage media on the local computer or on the network. Users might tend to keep their data files in many locations on the local computer or on the network. A library is a good way to collect all these folders in a central, easy-to-get-to location. One good reason to set up a library is to make it easier for users to find their data folders when these folders are scattered in different places. Another good reason to set up a library is to make it easier for a technician to back up data. When a technician uses the Windows Backup and Restore utility to schedule a backup of a library, all the individual folders in that library are backed up. In this lab, you will learn to examine the structure of a library, set up a library, and add folders to it.

ESTIMATED COMPLETION TIME: 30 Minutes

 Activity

Windows 7 creates four libraries (Documents, Music, Pictures, and Videos) by default and you can create your own. Three libraries (Documents, Music, and Pictures) are pinned to the right side of the Start menu by default and you can access these pinned libraries by clicking one in the Start menu. In addition, you can use Windows Explorer to manage libraries. Follow these steps to see how the default Documents library is constructed:

1. To open the Documents library, click **Start** and **Documents**. The Documents library opens in Windows Explorer (see the left side of Figure A-7).

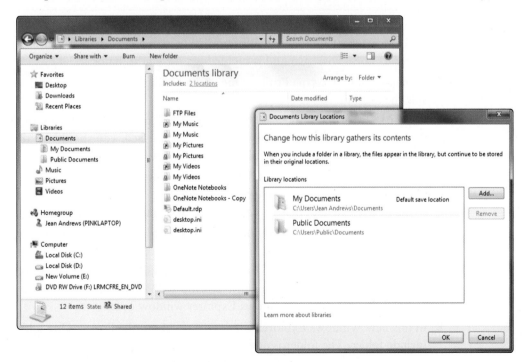

Figure A-7 Contents of the Documents library
Courtesy: Course Technology/Cengage Learning

A

2. At the top of the Documents library window shown in Figure A-7, it states that the folders and files are stored at 2 locations. Click **2 locations**. The Documents Library Locations window is shown in the right side of Figure A-7. By default, the Documents library contains two folders, the My Documents and Public Documents folders.

3. Click **Cancel** to close the Documents Library Locations window.

4. To learn more about the Documents library, in Windows Explorer, right-click **Documents** and select **Properties** from the shortcut menu. The Documents Properties box opens.

5. Notice in the box the check mark beside the My Documents folder. This check mark declares this folder to be the save location for this library. The save location for a library is the folder that a file will be stored in when the user copies or moves a file to the library. To change the save location, first select the **Public Documents** folder and then click **Set save location**. Notice the check mark is now beside the Public Documents folder and files placed in the Document library will now be stored in the Public Documents folder.

6. To make the My Documents folder the save location, select the **My Documents** folder and click **Set save location**.

7. Click **OK** to close the Documents Properties window.

Follow these steps to create a library with three folders:

1. To create a folder in the root directory of drive C:, in Windows Explorer, click **Local Disk (C:)** to select it. Contents of drive C: appear in the right pane of Windows Explorer.

> **Notes** If drive C: has been assigned a volume name on your computer, you might see the volume name beside C: in Windows Explorer.

2. In the title bar of Windows Explorer, click **New folder**. A new folder is created as a sub-folder to Local Disk (C:) and is highlighted for you to name it.

3. To name the folder, type **Project One** in the highlighted area. Then click somewhere outside the highlighted area.

4. Repeat Steps 2 and 3 to create two more folders in the root directory of drive C: named Project Two and Project Three. When you are finished, you should see the three folders listed together in Windows Explorer as subfolders to Local Disk (C:).

5. To create a new library, click **Libraries** in Windows Explorer to select it. The libraries appear in the right pane of Windows Explorer.

6. In the title bar of Windows Explorer, click **New library**. A new library is created and its name is highlighted. In the library name area, type **Work Projects** and then click somewhere outside the highlighted area.

7. To add a folder to the Work Projects library, double-click **Works Projects**. In the right pane of Windows Explorer, you are told the Work Projects library is empty. Click **Include a folder**. A new Windows Explorer window opens.

8. In this new Windows Explorer window, navigate to the **Project One** folder and click **Include folder**. The folder is added to the library.

9. If necessary, click **Work Projects** in the left pane of Windows Explorer. The contents of the Work Project appear in the right pane (see the left side of Figure A-8).

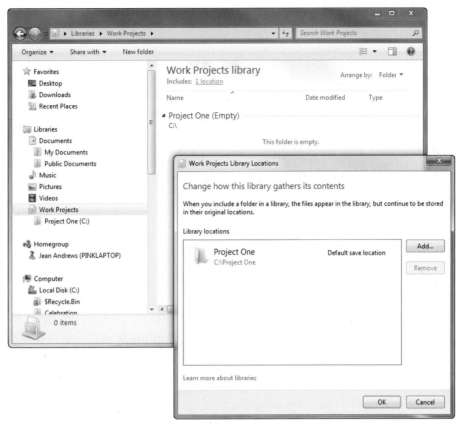

Figure A-8 Add a folder to the Work Projects library
Courtesy: Course Technology/Cengage Learning

10. At the top of the right pane, click **1 location**. The Work Projects Library Locations dialog box opens (see the right side of Figure A-8).

11. To add a folder to the library, click **Add**. A new Windows Explorer window opens. Navigate to the **Project Two** folder and click **Include folder**.

12. Repeat Step 11 to add the **Project Three** folder to the Work Projects library. The library now has three folders.

13. Click **OK** to close the Work Projects Library Locations box. Close Windows Explorer.

REVIEW QUESTIONS

1. Which four libraries does Windows 7 create by default?

2. Which two folders are included in the Documents library by default?

3. Which dialog box is used to change the save location of a library?

4. What are the steps to create a new library?

A

LAB 1.5 DOWNLOAD AND USE MICROSOFT SECURITY ESSENTIALS

OBJECTIVES

The goal of this lab is to help you learn how to use Microsoft Security Essentials to protect a computer from malware including viruses, spyware, rootkits, and worms. After completing this lab, you will be able to:

▲ Download and install Microsoft Security Essentials

▲ Configure and use Microsoft Security Essentials

MATERIALS REQUIRED

This lab will require the following:

▲ Windows 7 operating system, any edition

▲ Internet access

LAB PREPARATION

Before the lab begins, the instructor or lab assistant needs to do the following:

▲ Verify that Windows starts with no errors

▲ Verify that Internet access is available

ACTIVITY BACKGROUND

As a PC support technician, you need to make certain that every computer you support has antivirus software installed and is configured to receive automatic updates and to run in the background. Many free and paid-by-subscription antivirus software products are available and can be downloaded from the Internet. Among the free products, Microsoft Security Essentials is well rated and does a good job of protecting a system against malware. In this lab, you will learn to download the software, install it, configure it, and make sure it is running in the background to protect a system against malware.

ESTIMATED COMPLETION TIME: 20 Minutes

 Activity

> **Notes** Web sites change from time to time, so you might need to adjust the following steps to accommodate Microsoft changes to its site.

Follow these steps to download and install Microsoft Security Essentials:

1. Log on to Windows using an account with administrative privileges.
2. Using your browser, navigate to this URL:

   www.microsoft.com/security_essentials
3. Click **Download Now**.
4. To save the file to your Windows desktop, in the File Download - Security Warning box, click **Save**. The Save As box appears. Navigate to the **Desktop** as the save location and click **Save**. If you have a 32-bit version of Windows 7 installed, the file mssefullinstall-x86fre-en-us-vista-win7.exe downloads to the desktop. If you have a

64-bit version of Windows 7 installed, the file mssefullinstall-amd64fre-en-us-vista-win7.exe downloads to the desktop. When the download is complete, click **Close** to close the Download complete box.

5. Close your browser.

6. Double-click the downloaded file on your desktop. If necessary, respond to the UAC box.

7. The Microsoft Security Essentials window appears. Click **Next**.

8. On the next screen, click **I accept** to agree to the license agreement.

9. On the next screen, click **Validate** so that the program can validate your Windows 7 license.

10. On the next screen, click **Install**.

11. On the next screen, uncheck **Scan my computer for potential threats after getting the latest updates**. Click **Finish**.

12. The Microsoft Security Essentials window opens with the Update tab active and the update process automatically started. This process installs the latest virus and spyware definitions and then scans your computer for malware. Wait for the entire process to complete, which might take several minutes.

13. Click the **Home** tab. On the Home tab, look for the large green check mark on the page, which indicates the software is configured to automatically scan for malware and the software is up to date (see Figure A-9).

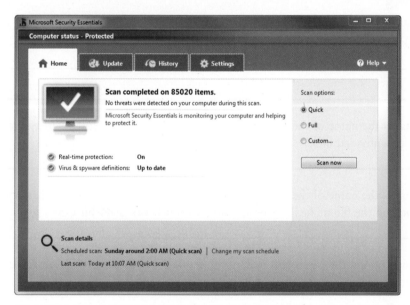

Figure A-9   Microsoft Security Essentials is up to date with the latest virus and spyware definitions
Courtesy: Course Technology/Cengage Learning

14. Click the **History** tab. List below any suspicious items the scan recorded:

_____

_____

_____

15. Click the **Settings** tab. Answer the following questions:
   ◢ On what day of the week and time of day is a scan scheduled?

_____

A

◢ Is the software configured to check for the latest updates before running a scan?

_____

16. Click **Real-time protection.** What is the purpose of having real-time protection enabled?

_____

_____

17. List the steps to configure the software to scan removable drives:

_____

_____

_____

18. Close the Microsoft Security Essentials window.

19. To clean up your desktop, delete the downloaded file, which will be **mssefullinstall-x86fre-en-us-vista-win7.exe** for a 32-bit system or **mssefullinstall-amd64fre-en-us-vista-win7.exe** for a 64-bit system.

REVIEW QUESTIONS

1. During this lab, what were the purposes of the two new icons added to your Windows desktop?

_____

_____

2. What is the name of the executable program file for Microsoft Security Essentials (not the downloaded file)?

_____

3. What is the name of the file you downloaded to install Microsoft Security Essentials? Based on the file name, is your system a 32-bit OS or a 64-bit OS?

_____

4. Which tab on the Microsoft Security Essentials window do you use to find out the Virus definitions version and the Spyware definitions version?

_____

LAB 1.6 INSTALL AND USE WINDOWS XP MODE AND WINDOWS VIRTUAL PC

OBJECTIVES

The goal of this lab is to help you learn how to install and use Windows XP Mode and Windows Virtual PC to run legacy software that normally would not run in Windows 7. After completing this lab, you will be able to:

◢ Download and install Windows XP Mode and Windows Virtual PC to create a Windows XP Professional system in a virtual machine

◢ Use Windows XP Mode to run legacy software

MATERIALS REQUIRED

This lab will require the following:

- Windows 7 operating system, Ultimate or Professional edition
- Internet access

LAB PREPARATION

Before the lab begins, the instructor or lab assistant needs to do the following:

- Verify that Windows starts with no errors.
- Verify that Internet access is available.
- Determine the key to press to enter BIOS setup. The student might be required to change a BIOS setting to enable hardware-assisted virtualization (HAV).
- Because the download time for the Windows XP Mode software can be more than 30 minutes, it is strongly recommended that the Windows XP Mode file be downloaded prior to the lab and made available to students. The file is named WindowsXPMode_en-us.exe and can be found at this URL:

  www.microsoft.com/windows/virtual-pc/download.aspx

ACTIVITY BACKGROUND

As with previous versions of Windows, you can download and install for free the Windows Virtual PC software from Microsoft. The software can then be used to create a virtual computer or virtual machine (VM) that simulates the hardware of a physical computer. You can install and run multiple operating systems at the same time on a PC, each working in its own VM. (Each operating system you install requires a license and product key.) These multiple instances of operating systems can be used to train users and run legacy software, and for support technicians to support multiple operating systems. For example, help desk technicians can run a VM for each OS they support on a single PC and quickly and easily switch from one OS to another by clicking a window.

Windows 7 Professional, Ultimate, and Enterprise editions offer the ability to install a fully functioning version of Windows XP Professional in a VM without having to own a license for Windows XP. The installation is called Windows XP Mode, and you can use it to run legacy software that normally would not work in Windows 7. For a system to qualify for Windows XP Mode, you need either the Professional, Ultimate, or Enterprise edition of Windows 7. In addition, your CPU must support hardware-assisted virtualization (HAV), and this feature must be enabled in BIOS setup or you must download and install a patch to override the use of HAV. Most computers made after 2007 support HAV.

When considering the use of Windows XP Mode, realize there are advantages and disadvantages. An advantage is that you can run older software in Windows 7 so that you do not need to purchase up-to-date software compatible with Windows 7. The disadvantage is the drain on system resources. Running Windows XP Mode can cause the entire Windows 7 system to run slowly and might mean you need to install extra RAM. To prevent this drain on resources, first try to run the legacy software using compatibility mode. Compatibility mode might work and does not use as many system resources as Windows XP Mode. How to use Compatibility Mode is covered in Chapter 1.

In this lab, you will learn how to set up Windows XP Mode to run legacy software. First, you will download and install Windows XP Mode in your Windows 7 system. Next, you will download and install Windows Virtual PC. Then you will set up Windows XP Professional in the VM for first use. Finally, you will install legacy software in the Windows XP Mode environment.

If your system supports hardware-assisted virtualization (HAV) and it is not enabled in BIOS setup, you must access BIOS setup and enable the feature. In this situation, you will need to know the key to press during the boot to access BIOS setup. Ask your lab instructor for this key.

A

Write down the key to press during the boot to access BIOS setup:

During this lab, you are asked to download the file, WindowsXPMode_en-us.exe, to your PC from the Microsoft Web site. The download can take 30 minutes to 1 hour depending on your download speed. To avoid waiting for the download, your instructor might provide the file. Ask your instructor if the file is already available in the lab. If so, record its location here:

ESTIMATED COMPLETION TIME: 90 Minutes

 Activity

Part 1: Determine if your system qualifies for Windows Virtual PC and Windows XP Mode

Follow these steps to determine if your edition of Windows 7 qualifies for Windows Virtual PC and Windows XP Mode:

1. To find out the edition of Windows 7 you are using, click **Start**, right-click **Computer**, and select **Properties** from the shortcut menu. The System window opens, which shows the Windows edition and system type installed.

   Answer these questions:

   ◢ Write down the edition you are using (Ultimate or Professional):

   ◢ Write down the system type you are using (32-bit or 64-bit):

2. Close the System window.

> **Notes** Web sites change from time to time, so you might need to adjust the following steps to accommodate Microsoft changes to its site.

To find out if your computer supports HAV, follow these steps:

1. Open your browser and navigate to this URL:

   www.microsoft.com/windows/virtual-pc/support

2. The Web page shown in Figure A-10 is your central location for information about Windows Virtual PC and Windows XP Mode. To bookmark the page in Internet Explorer, click **Favorites** and click **Add to Favorites**. In the Add a Favorite box, click **Add**.

3. Click the link **Configure BIOS**. On the next page, click the link **Hardware-Assisted Virtualization Detection Tool**.

4. On the next page, scroll down toward the bottom of the page to the area labeled *Files in This Download*. To the right of the filename *havdetectiontool.exe*, click **Download**.

5. In the File Download - Security Warning box, click **Run**.

6. In the Internet Explorer - Security Warning box, click **Run**. If necessary, respond to the UAC box.

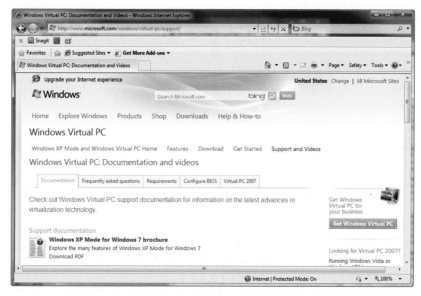

Figure A-10   Microsoft support site for Windows Virtual PC and Windows XP Mode
Courtesy: Course Technology/Cengage Learning

7. The Hardware-Assisted Virtualization Detection Tool window appears. Check **I accept the license term** and click **Next**. The tool runs and reports one of three possibilities:

◢ If your hardware supports HAV and it is enabled in BIOS, the box in Figure A-11 appears.

◢ If your hardware supports HAV and it is not enabled in BIOS, the box in Figure A-12 appears.

◢ If your hardware does not support HAV, the box in Figure A-13 appears.

Figure A-11   HAV is enabled and ready to use
Courtesy: Course Technology/Cengage Learning

A

Figure A-12 HAV needs to be enabled in BIOS setup
Courtesy: Course Technology/Cengage Learning

Figure A-13 The CPU does not support HAV
Courtesy: Course Technology/Cengage Learning

Answer the following questions:

◢ Write down the title line in the dialog box that appeared on your computer:

_____

◢ Does your CPU support hardware-assisted virtualization (HAV)?

_____

◢ If so, does the feature need to be enabled in BIOS setup?

_____

If your CPU does not support HAV, you can still use Windows Virtual PC and Windows XP Mode by installing a Microsoft fix after Windows Virtual PC is installed. If your CPU does not support HAV or your CPU supports HAV and the feature is enabled, proceed to Part 3 of this lab, skipping Part 2. If your CPU supports HAV and it is not enabled, proceed to Part 2 to enable it before you continue with the rest of the lab.

Part 2: Enable hardware-assisted virtualization in BIOS setup

In this part of the lab, you will need to know the key to press to enter BIOS setup during the boot. Follow these steps to change BIOS setup so that HAV is enabled:

1. What is the key to press to enter BIOS setup during the boot? Write down that key here:

   _____

2. Shut down your computer. Press the power button to boot up the system. Hold down the key to access BIOS setup. The BIOS setup opening menu appears.

3. Each motherboard manufacturer organizes the BIOS setup screens differently, so you might have to search a bit to find the screen to enable hardware-assisted virtualization. For one BIOS setup, the screen in Figure A-14 is used. Notice in the figure, the technology is called VT (virtualization technology) rather than HAV. For this BIOS, make sure **Intel ® VT** is set to **Enable**.

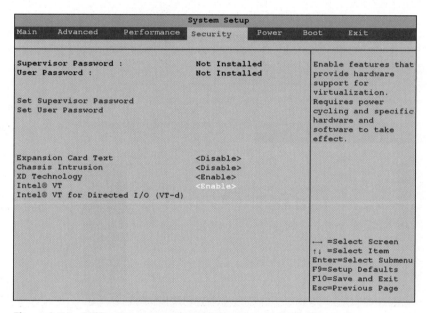

Figure A-14   BIOS setup screen to enable hardware virtualization
Courtesy: Course Technology/Cengage Learning

4. Also verify that all subcategories under the main category for hardware virtualization are enabled.

5. After you have made your changes, exit BIOS setup, saving your changes. How to do that differs for each BIOS setup utility. Ask your instructor if you need help.

6. Restart the system to the Windows 7 desktop.

Part 3: Download the Windows XP Mode installation file

If your instructor has provided you the downloaded file to install Windows XP Mode, skip this section and proceed to Part 4 to install Windows XP Mode.

Follow these steps to download the Windows XP Mode installation file:

1. Open your browser. Click **Favorites** and then click **Windows Virtual PC Documentation and Videos** in your Favorites list. The Microsoft support page for Windows Virtual PC appears in your browser window.

2. Click the link **Get Windows Virtual PC**.

3. A new browser window opens. Under Step 2 on this page, select your operating system and system type from the drop-down list. You obtained this information earlier in the lab. Be sure you select the correct option from the drop-down list.

4. Also under Step 2 on this page, select your language from the drop-down list.

5. Under Step 3 on this page, click **Windows XP Mode**.

6. The *Windows validation required* message appears. Microsoft wants to validate you are running a genuine copy of Windows. Click **Continue**. In the File Download-Security Warning box, click **Run**. If necessary, respond to the UAC box. If necessary, follow the directions on-screen to download and install an update package. Then click **Continue** again.

7. If a message appears above the page informing you that Internet Explorer has blocked a file download, click the message area above the page and point to **File Download Blocked** from the menu that displays. Then click **Download File** as shown in Figure A-15.

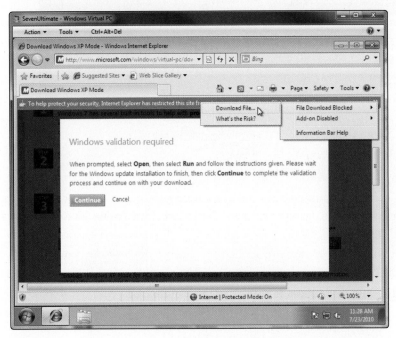

Figure A-15   Internet Explorer has blocked content from being downloaded to your PC
Courtesy: Course Technology/Cengage Learning

8. In the File Download-Security Warning box, click **Run**. If necessary, respond to the UAC box. If necessary, follow the directions on-screen to download and install an update package again.

9. If another message appears above the page in Internet Explorer, this one asking permission to run an add-on, click in the message area and select **Run Add-on** from the menu that appears. Click **Run** in the Internet Explorer-Security Warning box to allow the Active-X add-on to run.

10. A message appears saying Windows validation was successful. Click **Continue**.

11. Yet even one more message appears above the page saying that Internet Explorer has blocked a download. Click in the message area to display a menu and then click **Download File** in the menu. Then click **Continue**.

12. You are now ready to save the Windows XP Mode software to your desktop. In the File Download-Security Warning box, click **Save**. The Save As box appears. Select the **Desktop** as the location to save the file and then click **Save**. The file, WindowsXPMode_en-us.exe, downloads, which can take several minutes depending on your download speed.

13. When the download completes, click **Close** to close the Download Complete box.

14. Close your browser.

Part 4: Install Windows XP Mode and Windows Virtual PC

Follow these steps to install Windows XP Mode, using the installation file you previously downloaded or one provided by your instructor:

1. If your instructor provided the installation file **WindowsXPMode_en-us.exe**, copy it to your Windows desktop.

2. Locate the file **WindowsXPMode_en-us.exe** on the Windows desktop and double-click it. In the Open File - Security Warning box, click **Run**.

3. The file self-extracts and the Windows XP Mode window appears. Click **Next**.

4. On the next window, click **Next** to accept the default install location of the program. The install process begins. If necessary, respond to the UAC box. Wait for the installation to complete and then click **Finish**.

Follow these steps to download and install the Windows Virtual PC software:

1. Open your browser. Click **Favorites** and then click **Windows Virtual PC Documentation and Videos** in your Favorites list. The Microsoft support page for Windows Virtual PC appears in your browser window.

2. Click the link **Get Windows Virtual PC**.

3. Under Step 2 on the next page, select your operating system and system type from the drop-down list. You obtained this information earlier in the lab. Be sure you select the correct option from the drop-down list.

4. Also under Step 2 on this page, select your language from the drop-down list.

5. Under Step 3 on this page, click **Windows Virtual PC**.

6. If the *Windows validation required* message appears, click **Continue** and follow the directions on-screen and steps given earlier in this lab to download and run the Microsoft add-on to validate you are using a genuine copy of Windows 7.

7. If another message appears above the page saying that Internet Explorer has blocked a download, click in the message area to display a menu and then click **Download File** in the menu. Then click **Continue**.

8. To download the Windows Virtual PC installation file to the Windows desktop, in the File Download box, click **Save**. In the Save As box, navigate to the desktop as the save location and then click **Save**. The file Windows6.1-KB958559-x86.msu (for 32-bit systems) or Windows6.1-KB958559-x64.msu (for 64-bit systems) downloads to your desktop.

9. When the download is finished, click **Close** to close the dialog box. Minimize the Internet Explorer window.

10. Locate the file **Windows6.1-KB958559-x86.msu** or **Windows6.1-KB958559-x64.msu** on the Windows desktop and double-click it. In the Windows Update Standalone Installer box, click **Yes**.

11. On the next window, click **I Accept** to accept the license agreement. The software installs. When the installation completes, click **Restart Now**. The system restarts.

A

Part 5: Download and install the fix when hardware-assisted virtualization is not a feature of your CPU

If you determined earlier in the lab that your CPU does not support hardware-assisted virtualization (HAV), follow these steps to apply the fix Microsoft offers for this problem:

1. Open your browser. Click **Favorites** and then click **Windows Virtual PC Documentation and Videos** in your Favorites list. The Microsoft support page for Windows Virtual PC appears in your browser window.

2. Click the link **Get Windows Virtual PC**.

3. Under Step 2 on the next page, select your operating system and system type from the drop-down list. You obtained this information earlier in the lab. Be sure you select the correct option from the drop-down list.

4. Also under Step 2 on this page, select your language from the drop-down list.

5. Under Step 3 on this page, click **Windows XP Mode update**.

6. In the File Download box, click **Save**. In the Save As box, navigate to the desktop as the save location and click **Save**. The file, Windows6.1-KB977206-x86.msu (for 32-bit systems) or Windows6.1-KB977206-x64.msu (for 64-bit systems), downloads.

7. When the download completes, click **Close** to close the dialog box. Close both Internet Explorer windows.

8. Locate the file **Windows6.1-KB977206-x86.msu** or **Windows6.1-KB977206-x64.msu** on the Windows desktop and double-click it. In the Windows Update Standalone Installer box, click **Yes**.

9. When the installation completes, click **Restart Now**. The system restarts.

Part 6: Configure Windows XP Mode for the first time

Follow these steps to set up Windows XP Mode for the first time:

1. After the system restarts, log on using an account with administrative privileges.

2. Click **Start**, click **All Programs**, click **Windows Virtual PC**, and click **Windows XP Mode**.

3. In the Windows XP Mode Setup box, check **I accept the license terms** and click **Next**.

4. On the next screen, notice the user name is XPMUser. Enter **password123** twice as the password to the Windows XP Mode system. Click **Next**.

5. Select **Help protect my computer by turning on Automatic Updates now**. Click **Next**.

6. On the next screen, click **Start Setup**. Windows XP Professional is installed within the Windows Virtual PC environment.

7. Close the Windows XP Mode-Windows Virtual PC window.

Part 7: Download, install, and run legacy software in Windows XP Mode

Using Windows XP Mode, you can install legacy Windows XP applications that will not run under Windows 7. Follow these steps to install a game, Zoo Tycoon Card Flip, by Microsoft that was written for Windows XP and does not work in Windows 7:

1. To open Windows XP Mode, click **Start, All Programs, Windows Virtual PC,** and **Windows XP Mode**. The Windows XP Mode-Windows Virtual PC window opens.

2. In the Windows XP environment, open your browser and navigate to this URL:

   www.microsoft.com/windowsxp/downloads/trials/zootycoon.mspx

3. On the Zoo Tycoon Card Flip Game Download page, click **ZooCardFlip.msi**, saving the file to your Windows desktop.

4. Double-click the downloaded file on your desktop to install the software. Follow the directions on-screen to install the software. After the software installs, it automatically launches so you can play the game.

REVIEW QUESTIONS

1. What is the name of the installation file used to install Windows XP Mode?

   _____

2. What is the name of the installation file used to install Windows Virtual PC in a 64-bit installation of Windows 7?

   _____

3. If your system does not support hardware-assisted virtualization, how can you use Windows XP Mode?

   _____

4. If legacy software does not work in Windows 7, what should you try before you use Windows XP Mode? Why?

   _____

5. Hardware-assisted virtualization might be listed in BIOS settings under another name. What is another name for HAV used by the BIOS for the computer mentioned in this lab?

   _____

A

Labs for Chapter 2: Securing and Troubleshooting Windows 7

Labs included in this appendix:

- **Lab 2.1:** Identify a Hard Drive Bottleneck by Using Performance Tools
- **Lab 2.2:** Demonstrate Homegroup Security
- **Lab 2.3:** Use Advanced File and Folder Sharing
- **Lab 2.4:** Create a Windows 7 Repair Disc
- **Lab 2.5:** Explore the Repair Disc and the Windows Recovery Environment

LAB 2.1 IDENTIFY A HARD DRIVE BOTTLENECK BY USING PERFORMANCE TOOLS

OBJECTIVES

The goal of this lab is to help you learn to use the performance monitoring tools in Windows 7 to identify bottlenecks in the system caused by the hard drive or the applications using it. After completing this lab, you will be able to:

▲ Use the Windows Experience Index

▲ Use the Windows 7 Performance Monitor

▲ Identify a hard drive performance bottleneck

MATERIALS REQUIRED

This lab will require the following:

▲ Windows 7, any edition

▲ Internet access

LAB PREPARATION

Before the lab begins, the instructor or lab assistant needs to do the following:

▲ Verify that Windows starts with no errors

▲ Verify that Internet access is available

ACTIVITY BACKGROUND

A problem with slow Windows performance can be caused by hardware or software. Key hardware components that can cause a bottleneck include the processor, memory, and the hard drive. Several factors can affect hard drive performance: the speed of the drive, the amount of free space on the drive, file fragmentation on the drive, hard drive thrashing, and applications that make excessive demands on the drive. In this lab, you will determine if the hard drive is a bottleneck to your system by examining all these factors.

Performance Monitor offers hundreds of counters used to examine many aspects of the system related to performance. Two hard drive counters you will use in this lab are the % Disk Time counter and the Avg. Disk Queue Length counter. The % Disk Time counter represents the percentage of time the hard drive is in use. The Avg. Disk Queue Length counter represents the average number of processes waiting to use the hard drive. If the Avg. Disk Queue Length is above two and the % Disk Time is more than 80%, you can conclude that the hard drive is working excessively hard and processes are slowed down waiting on the drive. Anytime a process must wait to access the hard drive, you are likely to see degradation in overall system performance.

ESTIMATED COMPLETION TIME: 45 Minutes

 Activity

The Windows Experience Index can give you a quick overview of any bottleneck that might be affecting system performance. To view the Windows Experience Index, follow these steps:

1. Log onto the Windows 7 system using a user account with administrative privileges.

2. In the taskbar, click the **Action Center flag**. In the small box that opens, click **Open Action Center**.

3. In the left pane of the Action Center, click **View performance information**. Answer these questions:

   ◢ What is the Base score of the Windows Experience Index?

   _____

   ◢ What component yielded this base score?

   _____

4. Click **View and print detailed performance and system information**. Answer these questions:

   ◢ What is the total amount of system memory?

   _____

   ◢ What is the number of processor cores?

   _____

   ◢ Will this processor support 64-bit computing?

   _____

   ◢ Is the currently installed operating system a 32-bit or 64-bit system?

   _____

   ◢ What is the total size of the hard drive?

   _____

   ◢ What is the amount of free space on the hard drive?

   _____

   ◢ What is the total available graphics memory? Dedicated graphics memory?

   _____

   ◢ Based on the information you have just recorded, what one recommendation do you have to improve system performance?

   _____

5. Close the Performance Information and Tools window that was opened in Step 4.

Performance Monitor can be configured to measure how well the hard drive is performing and works by displaying counters related to hardware and software components. Follow these steps to use the Performance Monitor to display two counters related to the hard drive:

1. In the left pane of the Performance Information and Tools window, click **Advanced tools**. On the Advanced Tools window, click **Open Performance Monitor**. The Performance Monitor window opens. (Note that you can also open the window by typing *perfmon.exe* in the Search programs and files box.)

B

2. If the triangle to the right of Monitoring Tools is white, click **Monitoring Tools** to expand this category. Under Monitoring Tools, click **Performance Monitor**.

3. By default, current activity of the processor information object is displaying in a line graph and the line is red (see Figure B-1). The list of counters currently selected for display appears at the bottom of the window. In the figure, the one counter selected is % Processor Time. You need to delete any counters you do not need so that you will not unnecessarily use system resources to monitor these counters. To delete the % Processor Time counter, click somewhere in the row to select it. Then click the **red X** above the graph to delete the counter from the graph. The graph is now empty.

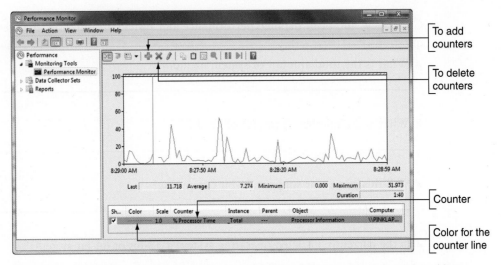

Figure B-1   Performance Monitor displays current activity of the processor information object
Courtesy: Course Technology/Cengage Learning

4. To add a new object and counter to the graph, click the **green plus sign** above the graph. The Add Counters box opens.

5. To add a counter for hard drive activity, under *Available counters*, scroll to and click the down arrow to the right of the **PhysicalDisk** object. The counters under the PhysicalDisk object appear and all these counters are selected. In the list of counters, click **% Disk Time**. This action causes all the other counters to be deselected and this one counter to be selected. Click **Add**. % Disk Time appears in the Added counters area.

6. In the list of counters, click **Avg. Disk Queue Length** and click **Add**. Avg. Disk Queue Length appears in the Added counters area. To close the box, click **OK**.

7. The two hard drive counters now appear in the Performance Monitor line graph. Answer these questions:

   ◢ What is the color of the line for the % Disk Time counter?

   _____

   ◢ What is the color of the line for the Avg. Disk Queue Length?

   _____

8. Keep the Performance Monitor window open as you perform other activities on your computer. In a real-life situation, you would open the applications a user normally uses

and work as the user would normally work to attempt to produce a normal working environment needed to monitor performance. In this lab, try playing a game or surfing the Web, keeping both the game and the browser open at the same time. As you work, watch the Performance Monitor window as it shows peaks in both counters.

9. Reading the counters by watching peaks is not accurate because the scaling in the line graph window might not be correct. To read actual values of the counters, mouse over the line and read the counter value that appears in a bubble window.

10. Performance Monitor also records the average, minimum, and maximum counter values under the graph. In the list of counters at the bottom of the Performance Monitor window, select the **% Disk Time** counter and answer these questions:

   ◢ What is the maximum value for the % Disk Time counter?

   _____

   ◢ Select the **Avg. Disk Queue Length** counter. What is the maximum value for this counter?

   _____

11. Close the Performance Monitor window and the Advanced Tools window.

Follow these steps to use Task Manager to identify a process that might be hogging hard drive resources:

1. To open Task Manager, right-click the **taskbar** and select **Start Task Manager** from the shortcut menu. The Task Manager window opens.

2. Click the **Processes** tab. Task Manager does not normally monitor disk usage, but you can configure it to do so. Click **View** in the menu and then click **Select Columns**. The Select Process Page Columns box opens.

3. Scroll through the list of columns that appear on the Task Manager Processes tab. Deselect all items that are currently selected.

4. In the list, select three items: **I/O Read Bytes** and **I/O Write Bytes** and **Description**. Click **OK** to close the box.

5. Any process listed in Task Manager that shows either the I/O Read Bytes column or the I/O Write Bytes column constantly changing indicates this process is hogging hard drive resources. Search the Task Manager processes for constantly changing values and answer these questions:

   ◢ List the processes that show constantly changing values and include in your list the description of the process:

   _____

   _____

   _____

   _____

   ◢ Of the processes you listed, which processes belong to Windows?

   _____

   _____

B

◢ Of the processes you listed, which processes do not belong to Windows?

_____

_____

6. Close the Task Manager window.

If processes that belong to Windows are constantly changing, most likely the problem is caused by hard drive thrashing. Hard drive thrashing happens when the system is short on memory and must, therefore, constantly swap data from memory to the page file and back to memory. This situation can best be corrected by installing more memory.

If a particular process that belongs to an application is hogging resources, consider upgrading or replacing the application with a more efficient version or product.

If you suspect the hard drive is a performance bottleneck, you might consider that there is not enough free space on the drive or that files on the drive are fragmented. Follow these steps to check these two possibilities:

1. A hard drive needs a minimum of 15% free space on the drive. Looking back at the hard drive information you gathered earlier in this lab, answer these questions:

   ◢ What is the total size of the hard drive?

   _____

   ◢ What is the free space on the hard drive?

   _____

   ◢ What is the percentage of free space on the hard drive?

   _____

2. Examine the hard drive and answer these questions:

   ◢ How much space can be cleared up on the drive by performing a complete disk cleanup?

   _____

   ◢ Describe how you found your answer:

   _____

   _____

3. Fragmented files can also slow down hard drive performance. If the default setting has not been changed, Windows 7 automatically defrags the hard drive weekly. Answer these questions:

   ◢ Is Windows 7 configured to defragment the drive weekly?

   _____

   ◢ What day of the week and time of day are scheduled for defragmentation?

   _____

   _____

◢ Describe how you found your answers:

_____

_____

If you suspect the hard drive is a performance bottleneck, you have adequate free space on the drive, and you have eliminated processes hogging hard drive resources, you might consider upgrading the hard drive to a faster or larger drive. Follow these steps to determine the speed of your drive:

1. Open **Device Manager**. In the Device Manager window, expand the **Disk drives** category. Answer this question:

   ◢ What is the brand and model of your hard drive?

   _____

2. Open your browser and navigate to the *www.google.com* Web site. Enter in the Google search box the brand and model number of your drive exactly as it appears in the Device Manager window. Click links to find the Web site of the hard drive manufacturer or other sites where you can find specifications for your drive. Answer these questions:

   ◢ Is the drive a solid state drive or a magnetic drive?

   _____

   ◢ If the drive is a magnetic drive, what is the RPM rating for the drive?

   _____

   ◢ Standard RPM ratings for a hard drive for personal computers are 5400, 7200, and 10,000 RPM. Do you consider your drive a slow, moderate, or fast drive?

   _____

3. Close all open windows.

REVIEW QUESTIONS

1. If you determine that the hard drive is experiencing excessive use, but the Windows Experience Index says that memory is the system bottleneck, which component do you upgrade first, memory or the hard drive? Why?

   _____

   _____

   _____

   _____

B

2. What values for the % Disk Time and Avg. Disk Queue Length counters of Performance Monitor collectively indicate the hard drive is a performance bottleneck?

_____

_____

3. Based on the maximum values for both hard drive counters you measured using Performance Monitor in this lab and the criteria for the two counters given in the Activity Background section of this lab, is it indicated that the hard drive is a performance bottleneck in your system? Why or why not?

_____

_____

_____

4. What can you conclude if a Windows process is constantly reading and writing to the hard drive?

_____

_____

5. How much free space does a hard drive need to prevent a performance slowdown?

_____

_____

LAB 2.2 DEMONSTRATE HOMEGROUP SECURITY

OBJECTIVES

The goal of this lab is to help you learn how a Windows 7 homegroup is used to provide security for shared resources on a small network. After completing this lab, you will be able to:

- Create and use a Windows 7 homegroup
- Change the homegroup settings

MATERIALS REQUIRED

This lab will require the following:

- Two computers using Windows 7, any edition, networked together
- A team of two students

LAB PREPARATION

Before the lab begins, the instructor or lab assistant needs to do the following:

- Verify that both Windows 7 computers start with no errors
- Verify that the local network is working

ACTIVITY BACKGROUND

Previous versions of the Windows operating systems support Windows workgroups to secure networked resources. Beginning with Windows 7, Windows supports both workgroups and homegroups. A homegroup is an easy method of sharing folders and printers on a small peer-to-peer network. The primary difference in a homegroup and a workgroup is that a password is assigned to the homegroup which applies to all computers in the homegroup. A user is not required to have a user account or password on each computer for accessing a networked resource. These rules make setting up a homegroup much easier than setting up a workgroup. However, with that ease of setup comes a decrease in overall security because anyone using a homegroup computer on the network can access a shared resource even if they are not an authenticated user on the computer sharing the resource. Using advanced sharing settings, you can, however, require that user accounts and passwords be used for controlling network connections.

In this lab, you and your partner will set up a homegroup between two computers and see how shared resources are managed by the homegroup.

ESTIMATED COMPLETION TIME: 45 Minutes

 Activity

In this part of the lab, you will set up two user accounts, User1 on Computer1 and User2 on Computer2. Follow these steps to set up a user account on each computer:

1. Log onto Computer1 with a user account that has administrative privileges.

2. On Computer1, open Control Panel and click **Add or remove user accounts**. Follow the instructions on-screen to create a user account named User1 that is a Standard user.

3. On Computer2, create a user account named User2 that is a Standard user.

JOIN COMPUTER1 TO THE HOMEGROUP

Follow these steps to set up a new homegroup or join Computer1 to an existing homegroup:

1. On Computer1, in the Search programs and files box, type **homegroup** and press **Enter**. The HomeGroup window opens. If the window reports the computer already belongs to a homegroup, click **Leave the homegroup**. On the next screen, click **Leave the homegroup** again. Click **Finish**.

2. On Computer2, if the computer already belongs to a homegroup, leave the homegroup.

3. To create or join a homegroup, the network location must be set to Home. On Computer1, to verify the network location, click the network icon in the taskbar and select **Open Network and Sharing Center** from the box that appears. The Network and Sharing Center opens.

The network location is reported under the category *View your active networks*. For example, in Figure B-2, the network location is a Public network.

B

Figure B-2   The Network and Sharing Center reports the network location
Courtesy: Course Technology/Cengage Learning

If the network location is a Home network, follow these steps to create a homegroup or join an existing homegroup and verify homegroup settings:

1. Click **HomeGroup** in the left pane of the Network and Sharing Center window. The HomeGroup window opens. If the window reports *There is currently no homegroup on the network*, click **Create a homegroup** and proceed to Step 2. If Windows detects and reports a homegroup on the network, go to Step 5 to join the existing homegroup.

2. In the box, you can select what you want to share in the homegroup. Select **Documents, Pictures, Music, Videos,** and **Printers,** and click **Next.**

3. The next screen provides a suggested password to the homegroup.

   ◢ Write down the password, being careful to record the correct case because the password is case sensitive:

   _____

4. Click **Finish.** Proceed to the section in this lab labeled *Join Computer2 to the Homegroup.*

5. If Windows detected a homegroup exists on the network, click **Join now.**

6. On the next screen, verify that the **Documents, Pictures, Music, Videos,** and **Printers** resources are shared with the homegroup and click **Next.**

7. On the next screen, enter the password for the existing homegroup and click **Next.** Then click **Finish.** If you don't know the password, go to another computer on the network that belongs to the homegroup, open the **Network and Sharing Center** window, click **HomeGroup,** and click **View or print the homegroup password.**

   ◢ What is the password of the existing homegroup?

   _____

If the current network is a Public network or Work network, follow these steps:

1. Click **Public network** (or if the location reads Work network, click Work network). The Set Network Location box appears. Click **Home network.**

2. Windows automatically wants to set up a homegroup for a Home network and displays the Create a Homegroup box. In the box, you can select what you want to share in the homegroup. Select **Documents, Pictures, Music, Videos,** and **Printers,** and click **Next.**

3. The next screen provides a suggested password to the homegroup.

◢ Write down the password, being careful to record the correct case because the password is case sensitive:

_____

4. Click **Finish**.

JOIN COMPUTER2 TO THE HOMEGROUP

1. On Computer2, verify the network location is a **Home network** and join the homegroup using the password you recorded in Step 3 above. Share **Documents, Pictures, Music, Videos,** and **Printers** with the homegroup.

2. On Computer1, still logged in as an administrator, open Windows Explorer. Under Libraries, click **Pictures** and notice the Shared status for this library in the status bar at the bottom of the Windows Explorer window.

3. To see how and to whom this library is shared, right-click **Pictures** and point to **Share with** from the shortcut menu. Then click **Specific people**. The File Sharing box appears. Answer these questions:

◢ What permission level does the Homegroup have for this library?

_____

◢ Based on the current Homegroup security, can a user on Computer2 copy a file to this library?

_____

4. Close the File Sharing box.

5. Using Windows Explorer, remove the Pictures library from the homegroup sharing. List the steps you did to accomplish this:

_____

_____

_____

_____

6. Still in Windows Explorer, click **Homegroup**. Record the resources you see available in the homegroup:

_____

_____

_____

_____

_____

7. Using Windows Explorer, create a folder under the C: root directory, naming the folder **\Data**.

B

8. Add the folder to the homegroup, giving the homegroup users permission to read and write to the folder. List the steps you did to accomplish that:

_____

_____

_____

_____

_____

Follow these steps to see how User1 can access resources in the homegroup:

1. On Computer1, log onto the system as User1.

2. Open Windows Explorer. Under Libraries, click **Music** and notice in the status bar this library is not shared with the homegroup.

3. Click **Homegroup.** Record the resources you see available to User1 in the homegroup:

_____

_____

_____

_____

_____

4. Based on what you have learned in this lab about homegroups, answer the following questions:

◢ Can any user logged onto a computer in a homegroup access resources shared with the homegroup?

_____

◢ If an administrator shares her Documents library with the homegroup, will the Documents libraries of all the users of this computer also be shared with the homegroup? Why or why not?

_____

◢ If one user on a computer shares his libraries or folders with the homegroup, will another user of the same computer be able to access these resources?

_____

5. Close all open windows on Computer1 and Computer2.

REVIEW QUESTIONS

1. List the steps to change the password to the homegroup:

_____

_____

_____

_____

_____

_____

2. What type of network location is required for a homegroup?

_____

3. What are the four resources that Windows includes by default in a homegroup?

_____

_____

_____

_____

4. In previous versions of Windows, a two-person icon on a folder indicated it was shared. How does Windows 7 indicate a folder is shared in Windows Explorer?

_____

_____

_____

_____

5. How many homegroups can you have on one local network?

LAB 2.3 USE ADVANCED FILE AND FOLDER SHARING

OBJECTIVES

The goal of this lab is to help you learn to use the advanced sharing and security tools in Windows 7 to give folder permissions to specific local users and to control a network connection sharing specific folders with specific users. After completing this lab, you will be able to:

▲ Configure how a network connection is controlled

▲ Assign folder permissions to local users

▲ Share folders with specific users on a network

MATERIALS REQUIRED

This lab will require the following:

▲ Two computers. One computer must use Windows 7 Ultimate or Professional and the other computer can use any edition of Windows 7.

▲ The two computers must be networked together

▲ A team of two students

B

LAB PREPARATION

Before the lab begins, the instructor or lab assistant needs to do the following:

▴ Verify that both Windows 7 computers start with no errors

▴ Verify that the local network is working

ACTIVITY BACKGROUND

In the previous lab, you learned how Windows 7 can use a homegroup to control the security of shared resources with a single password for each computer that allows it to join the homegroup. Sometimes better security is required when you want to control which users have access to specific resources on the network. For this type of improved security, you need to set up a user group for each classification of data and assign permissions to a folder or other shared resources according to user groups. Assigning permissions to user groups is easier to maintain than assigning permissions to specific users because you can add or remove users from the group easier than you can change the permissions on each folder.

In this lab, you will set up the security for a peer-to-peer network for a doctor's office. Two computers are connected to the small company network; one of these computers (Computer1) acts as the file server for the other computer (Computer2). You will create two classifications of data, Financial and Medical. Two workers (Nancy and Adam) require access to the Medical data, and two workers (Linda and Jose) require access to the Financial folder. In addition, the doctor, John, requires access to both categories of data.

Generally, here is the six-part process you will use in this lab:

1. On Computer1, verify the network location is set for a Work network and the advanced sharing settings for the network connection are configured correctly to use user accounts and passwords to control the connection.

2. On Computer1, create folders named Financial and Medical. Create five user accounts, one for John, Nancy, Adam, Linda, and Jose. All the accounts belong to the Standard user group. Create two new user groups, Financial and Medical.

3. Set the permissions on the Financial and Medical folders for local users so that only the members of the appropriate group can access each folder.

4. Share the folders on the network so that users in the Financial and Medical groups can access them from remote computers.

5. Test your security settings for local users.

6. For each user on Computer2, verify advanced sharing settings and test the access to both folders across the network.

ESTIMATED COMPLETION TIME: 45 Minutes

 Activity

Working with your partner, perform all four parts of this lab.

Part 1: Verify that the network location and advanced sharing settings for the network connection are set correctly

Follow these steps to verify that the network location and advanced sharing settings are configured so that user accounts and passwords are used to control the network connection:

1. Log onto Computer1 as an administrator.

2. Using the System Properties box, verify that the name of the workgroup is **WORK-GROUP** and name the computer **Computer1**. If you make a change, you will need to restart the computer and log in again as an administrator.

3. Click the network icon in the taskbar and click **Open Network and Sharing Center**.

4. A homegroup is available only when the network location is set to a Home network. To disable Homegroup security, set the network location to a Work network. To do that, look for the network location in the Network and Sharing Center under the category View your active networks (refer back to Figure B-2). If the network location does not show Work network, click the network location. The Set Network Location box appears. Click **Work network**. Click **Close**.

5. In the left pane of the Network and Sharing Center, click **Change advanced sharing settings**.

6. In the Advanced sharing settings window, verify these settings are selected:

   ◢ Turn on network discovery

   ◢ Turn on file and printer sharing

   ◢ Turn on password-protected sharing

   ◢ Use user accounts and passwords to connect to other computers

7. If you have not made any changes, click **Cancel** and the window closes. If you made changes, click **Save changes**. A box appears informing you that you must log off before the changes take effect. Click **Log off now**.

Part 2: Create folders, user accounts, and user groups

Follow these steps to create the folders, user accounts, and user groups on Computer1 (the file server) that is using Windows 7 Ultimate or Professional edition:

1. Log onto Computer1 as an administrator.

2. Create the two folders C:\Financial and C:\Medical.

3. To open the Computer Management console, type **Computer Management** in the Search programs and files box and press **Enter**.

4. Using the console, create user accounts for John, Nancy, Adam, Linda, and Jose. To create a new user, right-click **Users** under **Local Users and Groups** and select **New User** from the shortcut menu. Enter information for the new user and click **Create**. Make the password for each user to be the name of the user. The user will automatically be added to the Windows Standard user group. Click **Close** after the last user account is created.

5. To create the Financial user group, right-click **Groups** under Local Users and Groups and select **New Group** from the shortcut menu. The New Group box appears. Enter the name of the group and its description.

6. To add members to the Financial group, click **Add**. The Select Users box opens. Under *Enter the object names to select*, enter the name of a user and click **OK**. Add all the users that need access to this folder (Jose, Linda, and John). To create the group, click **Create** in the New Group box.

7. In the same way, create the Medical group and add John, Nancy, and Adam to the group.

8. Close the Computer Management console.

Part 3: Set permissions for local users

Follow these steps to set the permissions for the two folders:

1. Open Windows Explorer and right-click the **Financial** folder and select **Properties** from the shortcut menu. The Properties box for the folder appears. Click the **Security** tab (see the right side of Figure B-3). Notice in the box, that Authenticated Users, SYSTEM, Administrators, and Users all have access to the C:\Financial folder. When you select a user group, the type of permissions assigned that group appear in the Permissions area.

B

Note that the Administrators group has full control of the folder. Also notice the checks under Allow are dimmed. These permissions are dimmed because they have been inherited from the Windows parent object.

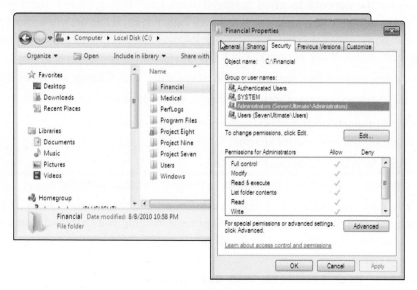

Figure B-3   Permissions assigned to the Financial folder
Courtesy: Course Technology/Cengage Learning

2. To remove the inherited status from these permissions so you can change them, click **Advanced.** The Advanced Security Settings box appears. Click **Change Permissions.** You can now uncheck **Include inheritable permissions from this object's parent** (see Figure B-4). A Windows Security warning box appears, also shown in Figure B-4. To keep the current permissions, but remove the inherited status placed on them, click **Add.**

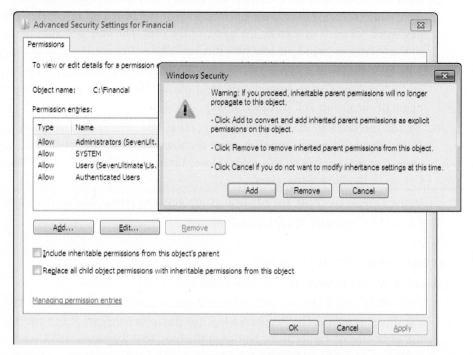

Figure B-4   Remove the inherited status from the current permissions
Courtesy: Course Technology/Cengage Learning

3. Click **Apply** and click **OK** twice to close the Advanced Security Settings box.

4. In the Financial Properties box, notice the permissions are now checked in black, indicating they are no longer inherited permissions and can be changed. Click **Edit** to change these permissions.

5. The Permissions box opens (see Figure B-5). Select the **Users** group and click **Remove**. Also remove the **Authenticated Users** group. Don't remove the SYSTEM group. Also, don't remove the Administrators group so that an administrator can access the data.

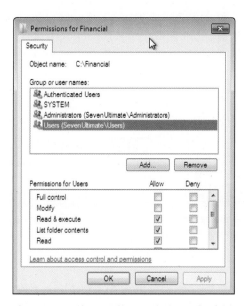

Figure B-5   Change the permissions of a folder
Courtesy: Course Technology/Cengage Learning

6. To add a new group, click **Add**. The Select Users or Groups box opens. Under *Enter the object names to select*, type **Financial** and click **OK**. The Financial group is added to the list of groups and users for this folder.

7. Using the check box under Permissions for Financial, check **Allow** under **Full control** to give that permission to this user group. Click **Apply** and click **OK** twice to close the Properties box.

8. Change the permissions of the C:\Medical folder so that Authenticated Users and Users are not allowed access and the Medical group is allowed full control.

Part 4: Share the folders on the network

So far, the folders have been assigned permissions so that local users can access them. The next step is to share the two folders so that others on the network can access the folders. Follow these steps to share the folders on the network and set share permissions for remote users:

1. Open the Medical folder's Properties box and click the **Sharing** tab (see the left side of Figure B-6).

2. Click **Advanced Sharing**. In the Advanced Sharing box (see the right side of Figure B-6), check **Share this folder**.

3. Click **Permissions**. The Permissions box appears. By default, Windows shares a folder on the network with everyone. Select **Everyone** and click **Remove**.

4. Click **Add**. The Select User or Groups box appears where you can add user accounts or groups that can access the folder. For the C:\Medical folder, we want to give access to

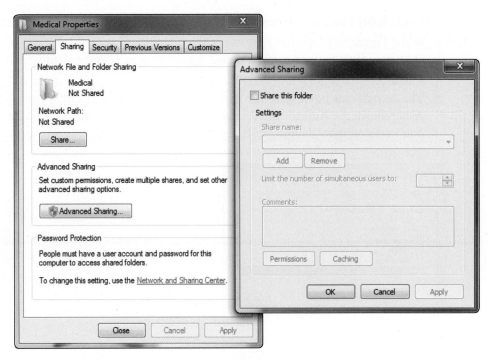

Figure B-6 Share the folder with others on the network
Courtesy: Course Technology/Cengage Learning

the Medical user group. In the *Enter the object names to select* box, type **Medical** and click **OK**.

5. Notice that the permission assigned the Medical group is Read. Check **Full Control** under the Allow column and click **Apply**. Click **OK** twice and then close the Properties window.

6. Now share the **Financial** folder and remove share permissions to **Everyone**. Add share permissions for the Financial user group, giving the group full control of the folder.

Part 5: Test your security settings with local users

Do the following to test the share permissions on each shared folder.

1. Still on Computer1, create a file in the Medical folder and another file in the Financial folder. Note that, as an administrator, you might need to respond to the UAC box to get access to these folders.

2. Log on as John and assign the password John to the account. Verify that John can access both the Medical and Financial folders.

3. Log on as Nancy and assign Nancy as the password. Verify that Nancy can access the Medical folder but cannot access the Financial folder.

4. Log on as Adam and assign Adam as the password. Verify that Adam can access the Medical folder but cannot access the Financial folder.

5. Log on as Linda and assign Linda as the password. Verify that Linda can access the Financial folder but cannot access the Medical folder.

6. Log on as Jose and assign Jose as the password. Verify that Jose can access the Financial folder but cannot access the Medical folder.

Part 6: Verify advanced sharing settings and test your security settings on the network for each user on Computer2

1. On Computer2, log on as an administrator.

2. Using the System Properties box, verify the name of the workgroup is **WORKGROUP**. If you make a change, you will need to restart the computer and log in again as an administrator.

3. Create user accounts for John, Nancy, Adam, Linda, and Jose. Make the password for each account the name of the user.

4. Use the Network and Sharing Center window to verify the network location is set to a Work network.

5. Log onto Computer2 as John and assign the password John to the account.

6. In the Network and Sharing Center, click **Change advanced sharing settings** and verify that these settings are applied in the Advanced sharing settings window:

   ◢ Turn on network discovery

   ◢ Turn on file and printer sharing

   ◢ Turn on password-protected sharing

   ◢ Use user accounts and passwords to connect to other computers

Note that if you have made any changes, you will need to log off and log back on as John.

7. Verify that John can access both the Medical and Financial folders on Computer1. If you have a problem accessing the folders, go back and check your work, making sure all settings are correct. If you still have a problem, try logging off and logging back on. If that doesn't work, try restarting both computers.

8. Log onto Computer2 as Nancy and assign Nancy as the password. Verify settings in the Advanced sharing settings window as listed in Step 6. Verify that Nancy can access the Medical folder but cannot access the Financial folder on Computer1.

9. Log onto Computer2 as Adam and assign Adam as the password. Verify settings in the Advanced sharing settings window as listed in Step 6. Verify that Adam can access the Medical folder but cannot access the Financial folder on Computer1.

10. Log onto Computer2 as Linda and assign Linda as the password. Verify settings in the Advanced sharing settings window as listed in Step 6. Verify that Linda can access the Financial folder but cannot access the Medical folder on Computer1.

11. Log onto Computer2 as Jose and assign Jose as the password. Verify settings in the Advanced sharing settings window as listed in Step 6. Verify that Jose can access the Financial folder but cannot access the Medical folder on Computer2.

REVIEW QUESTIONS

1. Why is it necessary that Computer1 run Windows 7 Ultimate or Professional edition to implement the security used in this lab?

   _____

   _____

2. When viewing the permissions assigned to a folder, why might these permissions be dimmed so that you cannot change them?

   _____

   _____

B

3. When assigning permissions to a folder, why might you include the Administrators group?

_____

_____

4. What is the difference between assigning permissions to a folder and sharing the folder?

_____

_____

5. What is the purpose of turning on *Use user accounts and passwords to connect to other computers* in the Advanced sharing settings window?

_____

_____

LAB 2.4 CREATE A WINDOWS 7 REPAIR DISC

OBJECTIVES

The goal of this lab is to help you learn to create a Windows 7 repair disc to be used in the event the hard drive will not boot and the Windows 7 setup DVD is not available. After completing this lab, you will be able to:

◢ Create a Windows 7 repair disc

◢ Verify that the disc boots without errors

MATERIALS REQUIRED

This lab will require the following:

◢ Windows 7, any edition

◢ A computer with a CD-R drive or other optical drive that will burn a CD

◢ Blank CD-R disc

LAB PREPARATION

Before the lab begins, the instructor or lab assistant needs to do the following:

◢ Verify that Windows starts with no errors

ACTIVITY BACKGROUND

Previous versions of Windows required that you use the Windows setup DVD to boot the system when the hard drive would not boot. Using the Windows setup DVD, you could then launch Windows Recovery Environment (Windows RE) to repair a failed Windows installation. Windows 7 allows you to create a bootable repair disc that holds Windows RE. The repair disc can be used in place of the Windows 7 setup DVD to fix a corrupted Windows installation. When Windows creates the repair disc, a 32-bit version of Windows creates a 32-bit version of Windows RE, and a 64-bit version of Windows creates a 64-bit version of Windows RE. These discs are not interchangeable; you must use a 32-bit repair disc to repair a 32-bit installation of Windows or a 64-bit repair disc to repair a 64-bit installation of Windows. You can however, use a repair disc created by one edition of Windows 7 to repair another edition. For example, a repair disc created by Windows 7 Home Premium can be used to repair a Windows 7 Ultimate installation.

In addition to launching Windows RE from the repair disc or the Windows 7 setup DVD, Windows 7 installs Windows RE on the hard drive. Therefore, in Windows 7, you have three options for launching Windows RE: the hard drive, the Windows 7 setup DVD, or the repair disc.

In this lab, you will create the repair disc. Then in the next lab, you will use the repair disc to explore Windows RE.

ESTIMATED COMPLETION TIME: 15 Minutes

 Activity

Follow these steps to create a Windows 7 repair disc:

1. To find out if your version of Windows 7 is a 32-bit or 64-bit OS, click **Start**, right-click **Computer**, and select **Properties** from the shortcut menu. The System window appears. Answer these questions:

   ◢ Is your system type a 32-bit operating system or a 64-bit operating system?
   _____

   ◢ What edition of Windows 7 is installed?
   _____

2. Insert a blank CD in your CD-R drive or other optical drive that has the ability to burn a CD.

3. There are several ways to launch the utility to build the repair disc. In this lab, you will use the Backup and Restore window. Click **Start**, enter **Backup and Restore** in the Search programs and files box, and click **Enter**. The Backup and Restore window opens.

4. In the left pane, click **Create a system repair disc** and follow the directions on-screen to create the disc.

5. Remove the CD from the drive and label it "Windows 7 32-bit Repair Disc" for a 32-bit version of Windows or "Windows 7 64-bit Repair Disc" for a 64-bit version of Windows. Also include on the label the edition of Windows 7 used to create the disc.

Follow these steps to test the repair disc, verifying that you can use it to boot the system and launch Windows RE:

1. Insert the repair disc in the optical drive and restart the system. A message might appear that says, "Press any key to boot from DVD or CD." If so, press any key.

2. If the system does not boot from the disc, chances are BIOS setup is configured to look first to the hard drive before turning to the optical drive for a boot device. Check BIOS setup and change the boot sequence so that it looks to the optical drive before it turns to the hard drive for an OS. How to access BIOS setup depends on your computer. Look for a message that says "Press Del to access setup" or "Press F2 for setup" or a similar message when the system is first started. After you have made your changes, save your BIOS settings and reboot. This time you should be able to boot from the disc.

B

3. After you have booted from the CD, the first screen shows the System Recovery Options window where you can select your keyboard input method. When you see this window, you know you have successfully created the repair disc and it is bootable. You can now remove the disc and restart the system to the Windows 7 desktop. Save the repair disc to use in Lab 2.5.

REVIEW QUESTIONS

1. Is your system a 32-bit or 64-bit operating system?

_____

2. Why do you think it is important to label the Windows repair disc as a 32-bit or 64-bit version?

_____

_____

3. Sometimes a computer boots directly to the hard drive even when a bootable CD is inserted in the optical drive. Explain why this happens and how you can fix the problem so that the computer boots from the CD:

_____

_____

_____

_____

4. What key on your computer do you press to access BIOS setup to change the boot sequence?

_____

LAB 2.5 EXPLORE THE REPAIR DISC AND THE WINDOWS RECOVERY ENVIRONMENT

OBJECTIVES

The goal of this lab is to help you learn how to use the repair disc and the Windows 7 Recovery Environment (Windows RE) to solve problems with Windows startup. After completing this lab, you will be able to:

▲ Boot to the Windows RE user interface using two methods

▲ Use the tools in Windows RE to solve startup problems

MATERIALS REQUIRED

This lab will require the following:

▲ Windows 7 operating system

▲ Repair disc created in Lab 2.4

LAB PREPARATION

Before the lab begins, the instructor or lab assistant needs to do the following:

▲ Verify that Windows boots with no errors

▲ Verify that the repair disc created in Lab 2.4 is available

ACTIVITY BACKGROUND

The Windows Recovery Environment (Windows RE) is an operating system designed to be used to recover from a corrupted Windows installation. Windows RE can be loaded from the Windows setup DVD, the repair disc, or the hard drive. It contains graphical and command-line tools used to troubleshoot a failed Windows startup. Follow along in the lab as you learn to use Windows RE.

ESTIMATED COMPLETION TIME: 45 Minutes

 Activity

If the hard drive is still healthy even when Windows will not start, you can load Windows RE from the Advanced Boot Options menu. Follow these steps to load the Windows RE operating system from the hard drive:

1. If necessary, shut down the computer.

2. Start the computer and as it boots up, press **F8**. The Advanced Boot Options menu appears.

3. On the Advanced Boot Options menu, use the arrow keys to highlight **Repair Your Computer** and press **Enter**. Windows RE loads and the System Recovery Options menu appears. Click **Next**.

4. On the next screen shown in Figure B-7, select an account that has administrative privileges from the drop-down list of accounts. Enter the account password and click **OK**.

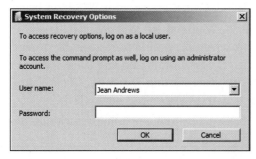

Figure B-7   Log onto Windows RE with an administrator account
Courtesy: Course Technology/Cengage Learning

5. The System Recovery Options menu appears (see Figure B-8). Click **Shut Down** to shut down the system. (You will explore the System Recovery Options menu later in this lab.)

B

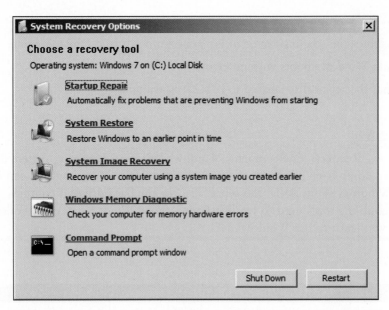

Figure B-8   The System Recovery Options window lists troubleshooting tools
Courtesy: Course Technology/Cengage Learning

The previous method of starting Windows RE from the hard drive will not work if the hard drive is corrupted. In this situation, you must use either the repair disc or the Windows setup DVD to load Windows RE. Follow these steps to use the repair disc you created in Lab 2.4 to launch Windows RE:

1. Insert the repair disc in the optical drive and power up the system. A message might appear that says, "Press any key to boot from DVD or CD." If so, press any key.

2. If the system does not boot from the disc, chances are BIOS setup is configured to look first to the hard drive before turning to the optical drive for a boot device. Check BIOS setup and change the boot sequence so that it looks to the optical drive before it turns to the hard drive for an OS. How to access BIOS setup depends on your computer. Look for a message that says "Press Del to access setup" or "Press F2 for setup" or a similar message when the system is first started. After you have made your changes, save your BIOS settings and reboot. This time you should be able to boot from the disc.

3. On the first screen, click **Next**. Windows RE searches for Windows installations.

4. On the next screen (see Figure B-9), Windows RE lists the installations of Windows it was able to detect. Notice on this screen the option to restore the system using a system image that you created earlier. Select your installation and leave selected the option **Use recovery tools that can help fix problems starting Windows**. Click **Next**. The System Recovery Options menu appears, as shown earlier in Figure B-8.

5. List the five tools available on this window and a one-line description of each tool:

_____

_____

_____

_____

_____

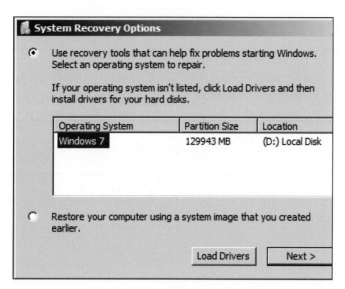

Figure B-9 Select your installation to repair or choose to restore the system from a system image
Courtesy: Course Technology/Cengage Learning

6. The first tool to try in almost every troubleshooting situation is Startup Repair, which examines key system files used to start the system and replaces or rebuilds them if a problem is detected. It's easy to use and you can't do any harm using it. Click **Startup Repair**.

7. The system is checked for errors and an error report is generated. Click **Finish** to return to the System Recovery Options window.

8. Click **System Restore** and then click **Next**. A list of restore points appears. In a troubleshooting situation, you can select the most recent restore point to restore the system to that point in time. The problem with using System Restore is that all changes to settings, user accounts, and preferences since the last restore point are lost. However, you can solve a problem with a corrupted registry, drivers, or Windows settings by applying a restore point. Applying a restore point is unlikely to eradicate a virus that has affected the system. To continue without applying a restore point, click **Cancel**.

9. Click **System Image Recovery** to completely restore the volume on which Windows is installed to the time the last system image was created. If a system image is found, information about the system image displays and you can continue with the restore. All changes to the hard drive since the image was created or updated are lost, including all user data, so use this option only as a last resort. If no system image is found, a message displays; click **Cancel** to close the message. Another window appears giving you another opportunity to provide the backup media that contains the system image. Click **Cancel** to return to the System Recovery Options window.

10. Click **Windows Memory Diagnostic**. A message appears saying that it wants to restart the system to test memory. Bad memory can cause corrupted or lost data and can cause Windows to become unstable, stop working, or intermittently hang. When you see these symptoms, check memory for errors. If Windows finds a problem with memory, replace the RAM. Click **Cancel** to not perform the test.

11. Click **Command Prompt**. A command prompt window opens where you can enter commands.

12. What is the default drive and path showing in the command prompt?

B

13. What is the command to list the contents of the current folder? Enter that command.

_____

14. What is the command to move up one level in the directory tree to the parent folder of the current folder? Enter that command.

_____

15. What is the command to close the command prompt window? Enter that command.

_____

16. On the System Recovery Options window, click **Restart** to restart the system and load the Windows desktop.

REVIEW QUESTIONS

1. What are the five options available in the System Recovery Options window of Windows RE?

_____

_____

2. Which System Recovery Option should you use to solve a problem with a corrupted device driver that was just installed and causes the system to not boot?

_____

3. When you insert the repair disc in the drive and restart the system, the Windows desktop loads. Why did the system not boot from the disc?

_____

4. Which System Recovery Option should you use if the system hangs at odd times and is generally unstable?

_____

5. What can you conclude if you cannot load the Advanced Boot Options menu by pressing F8 at startup, but you can load Windows RE by booting from the repair disc?

_____

_____

6. Which System Recovery Option will make the least intrusive changes to the system, System Restore or Startup Repair?

_____

INDEX